SO YOU WANT TO USE ROLE PLAY?

A NEW APPROACH IN HOW TO PLAN

SO YOU WANT TO USE ROLE PLAY?

A NEW APPROACH IN HOW TO PLAN

GAVIN BOLTON AND
DOROTHY HEATHCOTE

Trentham Books

First published in 1999 by Trentham Books Limited

Trentham Books Limited
Westview House
734 London Road
Oakhill
Stoke on Trent
Staffordshire
England ST4 5NP

British Cataloguing in Publication Data
A catalogue record for this book is available from the
British Library
ISBN 1 85856 196 5
(hb ISBN 1 85856 197 3)

Designed and typeset by Trentham Print Design Ltd., Chester and
printed in Great Britain by Biddles Ltd., Surrey.

CONTENTS

INTRODUCTION

This book has two kinds of readers in mind. Those of you who would like to try using role-play with your group, but don't know where or how to start. Those of you who, having tried it, now want to extend its scope and are ready to rethink its principles. Whether you are working in the caring professions, commerce, industry or education we hope these pages will offer you new ideas and a new way of looking at what it means to learn something through role work.

The book is full of examples of practice, but because we do not have a particular kind of group or learning context in mind, you should take our examples as representing a *kind* of role-play. We are not saying 'You should do this particular exercise', but rather, 'This *kind* of role-play may be suitable for what you are doing', leaving you to choose the subject-matter. So our chosen themes or topics are arbitrary. For instance, the first chapter offers a wide range of examples on Road Safety with young children. We are not setting out to appeal to teachers who happen to want to cover the subject of Road Safety with young children; we are using it to illustrate underlying principles of role-play that we hope are transferable to any topic you and your group are exploring.

Similarly we see our range of exercises relating to the theme of 'disloyalty' with adolescents, the training of apprentice gas-fitters in how to approach customers, the testing of managers in team responsibility and the medical students' initiation into visualising the daily responsibilities of the doctor they may one day become, as illustrative of principles applicable to a myriad of contexts.

But this book attempts to do more than outline the rules of role-play. Its authors have a mission! We are attempting to break what we see as the 'moulds' of role-play practice. Publications on the subject seem to follow one (or both) of two traditions. There is the 'simulation' tradition in which a 'real-life' work problem is replicated and the participants engage in solving it. Derived from this are a number of exercises set up to isolate for subsequent examination a particular deficiency in interpersonal communication. The learning outcome is to do with procedures and the effectiveness of individuals to follow them. The second tradition has a 'counselling' basis. In these the emphasis is on sensitivity in groups and the honest facing up to one's behaviour in stressful work situations. You will find that most recommended role-play practice derives from one or other of these traditions. Much of it is based on sound principles and planning. And yet anecdotal recollections of past role-play experiences often dismiss the work as a waste of time and/or a dreaded embarrassment.

In this text we have avoided the 'counselling' aspect of role-play altogether. We acknowledge its potential in certain circumstances – indeed some of our own past experience has been involved in therapy – but we want to give a firm *educational* basis to the approach recommended here. Our objective will always be 'what do we want them to learn?' Our methodology will combine conventional teaching resources and dramatic forms of presentation. The term 'role-play' inadequately conveys what it is we are about. In our view such a term misleadingly stresses the behaviour required of the participants. What *we* are concerned to stress is the making of meanings for contemplation. Let us try to explain...

Imagine a huge, dazzling white square of paper with a tiny pitch-black cross in one of its corners. Our attention would be arrested by it and we might feel impelled to 'explain it' to ourselves. It cannot be said that its meaning (or meanings) is located in a particular place. You can point with your finger to the white paper and to the black cross but you cannot point to the impact of the two together, out of which the 'meaning' emerges at the moment of your contemplation, and is indeed dependent on your contemplation.

We hope that this analogy takes us nearer to our purpose in using role-play or role *work* as we often prefer to call it. It is not what our finger can successfully point to that we are interested in opening up.

It is the emergent meaning that requires our attention. We want to take the focus *off* role-play as form of behaviour of interest in itself (to be 'pointed at'), and steer it towards a meaning-making act of contemplation. The meaning will not lie either in the role-player nor in the 'character' being played, but rather in whatever the whole context is – of which that role-player and 'character' are but part.

Thus the essence of this revised version of role-play coincides with the essence of theatre. Both are about 'seeing something *as* **significant**'. Just as in our analogy of a cross on paper, the object only has meaning if someone wants to give it significance, so all theatre is fundamentally about finding significance. If the curtain goes up in the theatre on an empty stage except for a toppled chair, the audience immediately begin to 'read' it as a toppled chair isolated in an empty space – and they will not be able to resist giving some meaning to it. Even an empty stage is filled with 'present absence' – and the audience 'hold their breathe'!

Now the role-play exercises in this book may on the surface appear to have little connection with a public theatre – indeed we are not interested, for instance, in getting people to *act* – but they are *rooted* in this one artistic characteristic of 'seeing something *as* **significant**'. **This is essentially *the dramatic* methodology serving an *educational* purpose**.

Thus when we write of *broadening* the use of role-play, we are attempting to change its basic focus away from a behavioural emphasis to the **sign**ing of meaning, but, further, we recommend the leader of a group always be aware of those important, alternative, non-role-playing, educational avenues, so that the dramatic presentation may flexibly operate as critical to, complementary to or even supplementary to other learning experiences.

The broadening of the methodology allows us to embrace two contrasted conceptions of the groups we work with. Traditionally, there is a group of people *from whom* individuals will be selected as role-players and each of these players will be required to adopt a 'character', ready to interact with the other 'characters' and be critically observed by the rest of the group. We have argued above that even within this traditional usage of role-play, our aim is to focus attention away from either the player or the 'character' being played to the meaning emerging from the whole context. But we will also from time to time change this conventional way of doing it by putting the *whole* class in role. In doing it this way, not only have we ensured that the class will now be audience to themselves, we have changed the basic conception of 'role'. Whereas in what we have called the traditional approach, role is seen as the representation of an individual character or type, in this approach we have further removed the significance of the individual in order to embrace the notion of a [fictional] *group* of people. They are to be artisans, employers, librarians, scientists, artists, children, parents, pedestrians, and so on, ad infinitum, in fact any group of people that could legitimately exist as a group in the 'real world'. Using this method, whatever happens in the fiction is going to happen to a social grouping whose only claim to an identity is that they *are* a group and can identify themselves as a group. They learn about what role-behaviours are required of them as a group; they adopt that role, as a group; they respond to whatever happens, as a group; they make things happen, as a group.

Our claim is that this group entry into the fiction can enhance the learning potential of the material. Effectively, in using this method you are endowing your class with a role that increases their power or ability to engage with the material being learnt or studied. From being your students, trainees, or pupils, by adopting their collective role they are *repositioning themselves* for engaging more effectively with the subject matter. The chances of enhanced learning are often increased too when you take a role yourself of someone who meets the fictional 'group'. That you are 'inside' the fiction ['teacher-in-role' it is commonly called] allows you a degree of subtlety in exposing nuances of information, a subtlety that would not normally be available to you.

The introduction of this innovatory practice into role-play opens up a wide range of exercises that could not normally find a place in a book on role-play. Of course the techniques for handling them are equally innovative, drawing on a set of principles only marginally linked with regular role-play practice. Throughout the following chapters attention will be drawn especially to those steps that need to be taken to initiate your groups into their collective role and to how best you might create your role, when you need to do so.

Having gone to some length in the above paragraph to explain this approach that may be new to regular users of role-play, let us re-iterate that we will also be using the traditional methods of having 'characters' represented by one or two members of the class, although we will advise on how to make this less threatening than has happened in the past.

A word should be said about what we are *not* attempting in this text. We have already said that we will not be giving a place to the use of role in therapeutic contexts. It should also be clear that we are not offering advice to *Drama* teachers. Although we have claimed that it is the potency of *theatre* that we are enhancing for the purpose of role-work, it would be inappropriate to see the exercises in this book as a basis for Drama lessons in schools. One of the distinctions that can be made between role-work and school Drama is that the former is almost entirely leader-controlled. There is no room for the play-making on subjects of pupils' own choice that goes on in schools, nor for those open-ended dramatic activities in which no-one knows what the direction or outcome might be. Where the leader of role-play hands over decision-making to the class, it is done so firmly on the leader's terms and within strictly laid out parameters. Likewise, this book will be of little help to Dramatic Arts teachers who see a study of acting with all that entails of 'building a three-dimensional character' as a core part of their course. Indeed we shall see that this book almost entirely dispenses with 'acting' as actors conceive of it. The only occasion when this is appropriate is when professional actors are hired as part of the training course. [Referred to below]. Interestingly, teachers of English Literature whose remit includes dramatic texts may find the kind of advice we give about approach-ing text through role-work very helpful.

In the first two chapters we set out, using some fifty exercises, to demonstrate all the different kinds (the different *genres*) of role-play – we won't have succeeded for one can always think of others. Our idea was to ask, 'If you start, where do you start? Is it possible to grade exercises so that one can choose just the level that is right for your class?' Gavin Bolton, during the summer of 1998, in workshops with the NATD conference and New York University experimentally invited his classes to invent exercises relating to 'disloyalty' [the second theme tackled in Chapter One] and to classify them into shades of complexity, identifying in the process what appear to be the basic criteria for judging whether one exercise is more demanding than another. He would like to thank members of those classes who will recognise some of their own ideas here and there in the book.

Whereas the first chapter has young children and adolescents in mind, in the second chapter we confine our exercises to work with adults. Those included in training of Northern Gas managers have actually been carried out by Dorothy Heathcote, although we have not presented a full record of what was done. Rather, we have examined some of the exercises used as illustrative of a variety of *genres*. In this chapter too we give firmer indications of what a *sequence* of carefully stepped experiences might look like. The chapter begins with a wide range of exercises that might be given to medical students whose ambitions lie in becoming general practitioners. We are grateful to Dr. Malcolm Rigler of Withymoor Village Surgery, West Midlands for reading the manuscript of this section. Through a series of exercises we attempt to challenge them to ponder for a while on what being a doctor means – a frame of reference some miles away from passing medical exams! The chapter closes with an account of training work carried out by Action in Management (**AiM**), an organisation set up to give training courses to professional, industrial and commercial groups using dramatic methods.

Chapter 3 takes a second look at all those exercises covered in Chapters 1 and 2 in order to tease out the major dimensions affecting choice. This is a key theoretical chapter which, among other things, brings out the essential connections between role-play and theatre. We give further examples of exercises, this time relating to children's Health Education, and to 'bullying'.

Chapter 4 examines the importance of 'Sign' in helping your class to 'read' significance into what they are presenting. We include an example of Chamber Theatre, a form of presentation for the conveying of the meanings of a text through the careful selection of Sign.

Part of this chapter includes an examination of how Shakespearean text might be approached. Some of the problems faced by teachers of English literature are considered at various points in the book.

In Chapter 5, entitled 'Who are you teaching?' we set out to show how not only do we have to take into account that our classes have their own characteristics, but they bring their own 'point of view' to whatever the topic is and to their expectations of role-play. Further, we demonstrate how the choice of role affects 'who they are' at a deeper social or cultural level, an aspect that is sometimes not taken into account. We note the positive and negative effects of using 'teacher-in-role' in this respect and we introduce the revolutionary approach to education known as 'Mantle of the Expert'.

Chapters 6 and 7 have a different bias from the rest of the book. In each of Chapters 1-5 our intention has been to illustrate a wide range of role-play methods, clustered round a variety of subject areas. Our first priority has been to compare one method with another, showing how different dimensions of being in role and the different ways of setting it up directly influence the kind of learning that can take place. As we said above choice of *topic* has taken second place. We discovered there is a limit to this approach. While recognising its value as a means of instruction, we became aware that something was missing. In practice, one does not go around saying to oneself, *'What are the different kinds of role-play?'* One is much more likely to find oneself asking: *How on earth can I teach such-and-such a subject?'* In other words, one arrives at choice of role work through the topic, not the other way round. Now this makes a subtle difference to your choice of exercise and how you set it up.

With this in mind, we decided to conclude the book with a topic rather than a method. We felt it needed to be a topic of urgent interest to a lot of people and one that might have pitfalls for the unwary. We therefore chose 'Racism'. And then we realised that if we are really to give the flavour of a leader 'thinking through' an approach to a subject, this is impossible to do unless we pre-select the kind of group that leader is going to be working with. One cannot broadly recommend a role-play approach to 'racism'; one can only recommend that *if this is the kind of group... then...*

So, we had to select a group. We were about to write a draft of Chapter 6 round Easter, 1999 when we heard on the radio a black teacher who had been subjected to a severe racial attack recommend that the only way to re-educate society is to start with four year-olds. This gave us a focus for the chapter which we extend to 'young children' rather than confining the work to pre-school age group.

We felt that we could only begin to do justice to the subject-matter if we were to add a second group to contrast with this one. We wanted it to be an adult group, so that the challenge would be quite different. We felt we needed to select an adult group that is required by the nature of their job to deal with racism. The obvious choice was the Police Force. This became our theme for Chapter 7. We are grateful to the Chief Constable for Northumbria for checking the draft of this chapter.

The structures of Chapters 6 and 7, however, are not the same. With the young children we tend to concern ourselves with answering the question: 'What are some of the ways in to this topic?' We see a teacher as regularly 'opening doors' on a positive attitude to mankind, not making a big issue of something called 'racism', nor tackling the subject in an intense 'crash course', but rather, seizing the chance, whenever it occurs, to feed a frame of mind that embraces tolerance.

With the Police Force, on the other hand, the need for a 'crash course' may be paramount. Thus we have laid out what amounts to our recommendations for a two-day course. We take the reader, therefore, step by step through a series of exercises which, we hope, will be cumulatively effective. Thus the chapter is distinctive from all the previous ones because we go through our thinking at each point in the course. It is the only part of the book in which the detailed *logic* of a progression of experiences is analysed fully.

Thus, if you are not particularly interested in either the Police or in 'racism', you should perhaps nevertheless glance at this chapter because of its structure. Combine this too with the concluding chapter, which, in part, carries out further analysis of the two-day Police Officers' course.

One of the strategies of role-work that may be new to traditionalists is the use of teacher or leader-in-role. Here and there in our illustrated practice we give examples of such usage, concentrating on how to make it effective and protective for the participants. In our final chapter we put forward a basis for the kind of signing behaviour required in presenting a role to a class, indicating its distinctive difference from stage-acting.

We finally summarise the book by considering, in the form of a conceptual framework, the range of learning objectives that role work might achieve.

CHAPTER ONE

EXAMPLES OF A RANGE OF GENRES (1)

In a knot of eight crossings which is about the average size knot, there are 256 different 'over and under' arrangements possible... make only one change in this 'over and under' sequence and either an entirely different knot is made or no knot all may result. The Ashly Book of Knots

We have tried to visualise who will pick up this book and, if they are inexperienced in role-play, what kind of help they will want to read about in the first chapter. We concluded that an overall picture of what is available might be the right way to start, so that when you choose your first role-play exercise you have a sense of selecting it from a repertoire of choices. We will do this for two chapters, chapter 1. giving examples with infants and adolescents; chapter 2 will give examples from work in adult training.

Any attempt at giving an overall picture has its hazards, for all it can do is show the different *kinds* of role-play. It cannot, at the same time, indicate the *order* in which the exercises should be conducted. So you should regard this chapter as offering *flavours*. In order to give these 'flavours' some coherence we have confined them to just two topics and two age groups.

That does not mean that you can only use the exercises if you happen to be teaching that particular topic with that particular age group – we believe the exercises to be adaptable to many other teaching contexts and subject areas.

Examples of dramatic *genres* available to all leaders/teachers using role-play: A. Road-safety with Years 1-4; B. 'disloyalty' with upper adolescents

Road Safety

Supposing you wanted to teach Years 1-4 about safety in crossing the road:

> A1. You may give your class some practical exercises in Road Drill by inviting them to agree that the line drawn in the hall is a pavement edge at which they are required to 'look left' 'look right' and 'left again' – having heard you talk of the dangers of not following the procedure.

This practice would amount to minimal simulation in preparation for practice on a real road. This kind of simulation is straightforward – as straightforward as it is likely to be limited in its effectiveness. Rote learning through actions certainly has an occasional place in education, but this is rote learning *without sufficient meaning*. It is not without its uses, but calls for a back-up of an additional kind of knowledge. Much of what we teach as parents and teachers is enormously significant for us as *parents* and *teachers*. Our children often lack the experience or the interest to make the learning relevant for themselves, failing, as one might say, to *own* the knowledge. We of course *tell* them it's important, but they remain outside that knowledge, even when they are given practice in how to behave. What role-play can often do is help raise the level of meaning for the child [or, of course as we shall see in the next chapter, the trainee doctor, or industrial manager, for simply *telling* the doctor about the required bedside manner or the executive about chairing a meeting may be equally ineffectual], to a new level of personal understanding.

You may think that the way to make the event meaningful is to get your class to simulate a child being run over. It might go like this:

> A2..Teacher to class: *Tommy, do you think you could be knocked down? How shall we show the car coming along?...and so on...*

This kind of enactment in which a road disaster is to be replicated will indeed also be a disaster of credibility. The fault lies in its directness [leave such realism to TV!]. If participants are to learn from role-play, it is more likely to be effective if the treatment is *indirect*. Indeed most of the discussion in this book will be on how to set up an effective indirect approach to whatever the material is to be examined. There are many kinds of 'indirect'. Some of them will appear as examples in this 'Road-Safety' section. One is to **shift the focus**. In 'Road Safety' the central, horrific meaning is to do with a child being knocked down by a vehicle. It is typical of most role-play that you are immediately faced with the problem of how to make it sufficiently believable to draw attention to the seriousness of the topic without it becoming too distressing. Shifting the angle on the material may help. Let us look at two examples that do this:

Shift of Focus

One such shift would be to adopt the rote learning of A1, but to concentrate, not on the required actions, but on taking one's pet dog across the road – an angle on road drill that might enhance your pupils' interest in the subject:

A3. Each pupil 'invents' a dog, gives it a name and makes it a bowl [just a simple drawing labelled 'bowl'] with its name on so that the bowl will locate each pet in space. The class will bring their 'dogs' to the 'line of the pavement' [as in A1 above] in the hall, and, with some children representing cars, making the appropriate engine noises, the dog-owners [and dogs!] learn to cross only when there are no cars or when the cars stop. More refined practice can take place using traffic lights or the bleeps of zebra and pelican crossings or traffic wardens or men with flags. Dogs are rewarded with pats from owners – or even sweets!

And a different kind of shift:

A4 Supposing, after trying the above Road Drill and once more back in your classroom, you build up a story about a child who, in spite of having done the Road Drill back in school, while waiting for her/his parent to meet her/him outside the school gate, suddenly runs across the road in front of a vehicle and is taken away by ambulance. You perhaps draw [match figures] the event on the blackboard, the class deciding with you whether it should be a boy or a girl and on a fictitious name [not, of course, a name of someone in the class – we'll call her/him K!] and the colour and kind of vehicle etc. Then supposing you simply take on the role of K's parent and proceed:

Teacher narrating: *And then, as the ambulance departed, K's mother/father arrived at school expecting to see K. at the usual spot...*

Parent to children: *Excuse me. I'm looking for K...S/he's always just here...Have you seen her?...*

Suddenly what started as building a fiction through narrative turns towards an incipient drama, happening *now*, in what we might term 'fictional now time', with you 'in-role'. But the 'now' is not the 'now' of the accident. It is the 'now' of interacting with the parent who does not know what's happened – and the children, *do know*. They *own* the information the adult does not have. From being story-makers the children turn into eye-witnesses. As they explain what happened the 'parent' may express disbelief, guilt, anger, anxiety and a sense of practicalities for organising getting to the hospital.

This interaction in role may last but a few minutes. Nevertheless it carries a potential for new understanding. The seriousness of the event is not seen in the accident itself but in the parent's reaction to it.

This kind of 'short/sharp/shock' role-play can indeed give the participants a new insight into the implications of an accident. It provides an angle and an emotional impact that one would not expect to be already part of young children's understanding. But its very brevity demands back-up which may take the form of no more than occasional references back to 'the accident' whenever the opportunity arises as daily schoolwork proceeds or it may involve further role-play. **Or,** you may want to plan an exercise which guarantees more sustained, deeper understanding. Let us look at A4 (immediately above) again. Let us assume that you have built up the 'accident' story as before, but instead of employing the immediacy of an anxious parent as a 'way in' to the material, supposing... :

A5 .... you invite your class to join with you in inventing the idea that the BBC or local radio want to make a special radio programme for Road Safety week, that you will be 'the person sent by the Radio people to interview witnesses' and that the members of your class will be 'witnesses' – who, of course, will base their answers on the 'story' you have already agreed on. You will ask such questions as:

Can you describe for the listeners where exactly in the town the accident took place?; What time of day/year? What road conditions? Who saw it? – can you tell the listeners what happened? I understand you were the police officer called in....Are you the doctor?.....Can anyone tell us about the family?....etc.

And to carry out A5 you will *actually* have a tape-recorder and actually record, so that it is there as a piece of work for relistening to and for others to hear. Additionally, you may invite the children to create your role – selecting the coat 'this BBC interviewer' will wear, making the 'BBC badge' for its lapel, and even helping you prepare the questions. Thus they *endow* you with your role as you will theirs by your introduction to the 'radio programme': '*I am at..., meeting people who have first-hand information about the accident at... I know all these people are witnesses or friends of the sad family or members of the police force and hospital staff...*'.

Notice, too, the difference in emotional tension between A4 and A5. In A4 your class are directly *confronted* with the 'anxious parent'. They are required to respond spontaneously to the *'presence'* of the tragedy of which they somehow become part. In A5, however, they are responding to an intellectual challenge, to turn their story-building into a 'voice' of witnesses. But their reporting will be in the past tense, telling their story in a different way, but retaining it *as* a story.

Both A4 and A5 exercises have required you to lead through the use of 'teacher-in-role', a device that considerably expands the scope and quality of the learning that may occur. We shall later be using '*trainer*-in-role' in our work with adults. The whole concept of 'role-play' is revolutionised once one recognises the availability of role-inducted experience. The potential that lies in your respectful '*Are you the doctor...?*', with its tacit empowering of the member of your group you are addressing goes far beyond any traditional pre-instruction typically phrased as '*In this scene, will you play the doctor?*'. But much more of this later. Back to our discussion of choice of focus.

You may want to take A4/5 further. You may see your class' current interest in road accidents [perhaps someone locally has been killed or your class have experienced losing a friend] as an opportunity to touch on bereavement. In which case:

A6. When you build up the story you also create a wall map of where it took place and you mark a spot where there is a lamp-post around which your pupils can stick tiny representations of flowers or teddy bears etc. And then you may invite each child to make a 'condolence card' to send to K's family. When finished, they will 'post' them in the 'letter box' [just a box with a slit]. Then, when they hear the 'radio broadcast' [as for A5 above], they hear a bit they had not heard before:

'*...The family have asked me to read this message they have sent....Thank-you for the lovely flowers left by the roadside...we shall leave them there till they really fade away...so other people with children will be especially careful at places like that...We would like to make a 'memory' book of all the cards and letters we received after the accident.* – and the cards can be retrieved from their letter-box, for displaying.

Or you treat may 'bereavement' in quite a personal way:

A6a. After creating the wall map with its marked lamp-post and flowers, you can build up with your class how they want you to represent a bereaved family member – they help you to decide what relation they want you to be; they discuss how you are feeling; they define a space in the classroom as 'your house'; they decide what you are in the middle of doing when they 'arrive'; they decide where the front door is – and you supply a piece of cardboard on which you draw a knocker or bell.

> The children call at the door, you invite them in and they show you all the cards they have brought – you can hand round milk and biscuits, if you wish!, for the visit has to be long enough for them to gather something of your feeling of loss and how you are managing.

Or you may simply prefer to introduce the topic to your class by posing it as a quick problem requiring quick answers. You can ask them to illustrate an idea, a concept or, as in the next example, an explanation:

> A7. Supposing you ask the children, sitting in pairs, to consider why K, in spite of doing our Road Drill, had suddenly started to run across a road. You might ask different pairs to volunteer to come to the front of the class to 'show' their solution.

Now what kind of acting behaviour do you expect from your young childen faced with this task? We shall in this book keep referring to showing of this kind as 'demonstrating'. They are *answering the question* and *indicating* their answers, rather than '*talking*' them. They are 'saying' 'This is how we think it *was.*' They are not acting or even attempting to claim 'it is happening now'. Your comments as you set up the showing will reinforce this notion of 'offering an answer'.

Thus A3-7 above are examples of indirect role-play, mainly achieved by **shifting the focus**. A markedly different kind of indirect approach is to give the material a theatrical **form**. What follows is but one example of doing this, but examples of **formal** treatment will crop up again here and there throughout the book.

Formal *treatment of the material*

> A8. Supposing you divide K. into six Ks and prepare to show a sequence of moments in the accident, the Ks spread out at the front of the class equidistantly from each other. K1 is to stand at the edge of the pavement, waiting; K2 is to start running; K3 is to sprawl on the

road; K4 (with 2 'ambulance' workers) is to lie on a stretcher; K5 is to lie in a hospital bed; K6 is being visited by 'parent'. When the six have tried out their positions, you explain: *I shall walk quietly behind each 'moment'*, and putting my hand on a *shoulder*, ask *what that K is thinking*. What kinds of things do you think K1 should answer? K2? K3? etc. In this you are putting the onus on the rest of the class to think through 'the moment' – and each K may choose from their replies or, of course, have his/her own response. Then, *with a sense of formality*, the sequence is repeated as a 'performance' – and may be done over again with variations if interest is sustained.

Notice the word 'performance' is used here. This has been quite deliberate, for it carries that special component of 'We are enjoying using a skill to do this well; how well we do it is part of what you, the audience, will also enjoy. We want you to grasp the account we are giving of an accident, but we also want you to enjoy what we have accomplished.

But, of course, it is not necessary to give this exercise this kind of 'performance' emphasis. You may prefer each repeat to be spontaneously different and the whole concentration of players and audience [*and* teacher] to be solely on how many different kinds of thoughts are passing through K's head. In which case the *aesthetic* effect may be residual.

Or you might try something totally different, an 'expertise' frame:

Mantle of the Expert *approach*

A9. You address the class as if they are adults: *I've heard that your firm is good at making posters that appeal to young children. I work for — —-Council and we're worried about the number of road accidents lately. It's five year olds* [the fictitious age chosen always younger than the actual age of the participants] *we're most worried about – there was an accident outside a school last week, a child was waiting for a parent who was a bit late turning up....They don't seem to understand the dangers the way older children do. Do you think you could do some posters for the council that would help these children*

> *understand...?* Each child with crayons and paper creates an 'accident' poster. As they work you go round stimulating individual children to tell you the meaning of the drawing.

The above, A9, is an example of what we shall call a 'Mantle of the Expert' approach, a dramatic way-in to a topic that invests the pupils'/students'/trainees' actions and discussions with a self-perpetuating source of authority, yet allowing them to feel that they are 'being themselves'. Thus in A9 the pupils are given, not just a *reason* for giving careful attention to the message of a poster, but a degree of tacit *expertise*. A more demanding version of A9 might be:

> A10. A duvet-cover designer requires help from 'experts' in road safety, She wants children's bed-covers and curtains to carry messages *'that will help all children – just as they go to sleep and just as they wake up – to remember to be careful crossing the road at all times'*. You, in your role as 'designer', add: *It can be words, pictures, signs and symbols, but it should be interesting and fit a duvet or curtain size.* You 'wonder' whether the Highway Code would be any use..... and you leave the problem with them.

One interesting ploy in using teacher/leader-in-role in this way is to take advantage of the 'absence' [as it were!] of your 'teacher self' when the 'designer' is interviewing the children, so that, when the interview is over you can 'return' [as it were!] with '*How did you get on with the designer?*' Thus a recapping or a refocusing of the task can occur.

But the telling difference between A9 and A10 lies in the potential for **acquiring new information**. Whereas A9 invites the children to make posters from what they know, in A10 the opportunity for seeking new knowledge is implicit in the task. The children now have to *study* as part of their role activity.

This now becomes a key factor in setting up role-play. Some of the above examples tend to be about **raising awareness**. As such the experience can be brief but, one hopes, significant. But there are a whole range of role-plays that can **teach new things**, that can add information, extend conceptual understanding and give a factual background to an issue.

The issue we are dealing with here for our first example happens to be 'Road-Safety' with young children, so let us look at what role-play looks like when it requires them to **study** the material as a 'Road-Safety' **project**. Such material divides into two kinds of in-depth topics: (1) a study of how congested roads create safety problems and (2) a study of the implications of an accident.

A11 Let's go back to our A1. and A2 in which you took your class into the hall to practise crossing the road either as themselves or with their 'pet dogs'. Suppose, instead, you invite your class to make stand-up models of motor-cycles, cars, vans and buses, stand-up figures of people and cut-out shapes of houses shops and schools ready for a big road you are making with a long roll of paper that is going to go either round the classroom or round the hall [removable when not in use!]. You will have marked your road with traffic lights, zebra crossings and junctions.

(1) The class first explore, as car drivers, where the best places are for parking, the safest places for pedestrians to cross and the places to be marked as 'blackspots', noticing too how parked cars can affect sightlines.

(2) On another day you could invite the children to examine the layout in which you have deliberately preset traffic and people into all sorts of potential accidents, which the children have to identify and report on or you could pose the question: 'How does a teacher organise taking a long line of children to pay a visit to the (fairly inaccessible from school, of course) local church?'

(3) Then in role as curators of the Road Safety exhibition at the Civic Centre, they demonstrate to you as a 'visiting teacher who wants to bring her class to the exhibition' what they would teach your class. They split into 'specialist' groups to do this, each group responsible for teaching about traffic lights or crossings or car speeds or pedestrians etc. and

(4) Role reversal – the 'experts' now take on a role as 'the visiting teacher's class' quite lacking in understanding the exhibition, so that you, 'the visiting teacher' have to teach *them*! – a wonderful way of pupils 'testing the teacher'! [It may well be worthwhile to complete the project by inviting a police officer in to school to give his professional perspective on their road model.]

If we move now to young children studying the accident itself. You could choose issues such as (a) all the different kinds of human error or (b) all the kinds of people involved when there is an accident and the procedures that have to be followed or (c) the work of professionals who were not actually there at any point who nevertheless have to understand what happened. Notice how this differs in intellectual demand from A4 above which merely invites the young children to 'build a story' of what happened. You are now setting up a *study project* for slightly higher grades.

A12

(a) Your class could draw a range of pictures of accidents (showing both examples of bad driving and of pedestrians [including dogs!] who need extra care) accompanied by written explanations of what happened in each instance, their explanations veering towards understanding not blaming, to be viewed as a 'gallery' by visitors who can be shown round and ask questions. [A more advanced version of this could require the class to create a Police TV documentary: *Matters of Concern: Road Safety*]

(b) You could assemble a picture or (preferably) a collage of an accident and require your class to identify all the various people who are drawn in to such an occurrence, including occupants of vehicles, passers-by, ambulance, police etc. Then you introduce the notion of inquest, enquiry or trial. In groups you ask them to be one kind of person involved and to prepare an account of 'what happened', ready for the 'hearings' with you in role as coroner, chairperson or magistrate.

(c) Or, alternatively, you could prepare some short 'evidence sheets' (perhaps written by the children prior to this exercise) e.g. *Eye witness: lady driver of car which stopped to help. Said 'I saw that the car which hit the person had only one rear light as it passed me.'* For now you will be in role as a senior police officer, ready to answer questions from 'the press' who are eager to get sight of the pile of statements in your hand.

And why not turn it into fun?

A13. A Road Safety Board Game [for Years 3/4]. The game could have all the usual counters moving up or down coloured, graphic squares as rewards and penalties, but some of the rewards could be based, not merely on the chance throw of the dice but on successful completion of a task, such as numbering the following 'police duties on-the-spot' in the right order:

> stopped all traffic
> measured the road
> used my mobile phone to summon help
> helped the uninjured passenger out of the car
> looked to see if anyone was hurt
> covered the injured person
> put out cones
> asked people what happened

We hope that the above 13 examples are useful indicators of the *range* of role-plays possible with any particular topic or any particular age group.

In this book we hope to examine what principles lie behind choice of role-play and choice of topic. Let us see what possible range of flavours would be available with a contrasted topic – and with, say, a group of young adults. Snatching a topic out of the air, let's choose, 'the meaning of betrayal'.

Upper Adolescents

The above examples are attempts to deepen a child's perception of a particular context of behaviour. As the child matures, we want her to go beyond the drilled skill behaviour to grasping some of the wider implications which will eventually feed into her becoming a safer cyclist and driver as well as a more responsible pedestrian. Sometimes role-play has nothing to do with acquiring a skill but is used to expand a person's understanding of an abstract concept to do with the nature of being human. Let us take as an example the concept of **disloyalty**.

Unlike 'Road Safety', there is no room here for rote learning. Indeed, it is difficult to enact a concept such as 'disloyalty' without inadvertently *reinforcing* the behaviour. We shall find this again in the next chapter when we look at problems of role-playing 'bully-ing'. So the learning outcome is one of *understanding*, but we should be aware that the very process could make 'bullying' or 'dis-loyalty' seem very attractive.

B1. The teacher/leader might instruct: *Turn to the partner sitting next to you. You are a retired person. You are going to recall an incident, now perhaps quite amusing but not at the time, when a mutual [fictitious] friend, betrayed you, say, by breaking a promise to keep a secret. Your partner may just listen or ask questions for amplification.*

The skill of setting up a role play lies in (1) defining the objectives (2) selecting an appropriate fictitious context (3) recognising what needs to be done or explained to lead into the first episode of role-playing (4) recognising the probable sequence of episodes and (5) giving the instruction for each episode in a way that makes clear the limits or *parameters* of the exercise

'Parameters' relate to both *content* and *social interaction*, that is, to both the intellectual demands and the interpersonal demands. A group of people required to do the above exercise may stay seated in the same grouping and with minimal shift of position; they begin to adopt either a narrator or a supportive listener function. Thus the *physical* rearrangement for the interaction is negligeable, signi-ficantly so, for the minimal change in physicality can feel protective to the inexperienced. The overall mood is one of *recalling* and the 'listener' has no vested interest in the anecdote.

Thus to the parameter of *social interaction*, there appear to be two major dimensions: *physical and emotional*. The exercise as des-cribed in B1. makes minimal demands in respect of each. *Physically,* the participants have barely moved. *Emotionally*, the 'listener' is required to offer no more than polite listening and the 'narrator' is but making up a fictitious incident. Of course, the very act of saying 'This is what happened to me' makes the emotional level, bland as it is, sharper than if you had merely invited the class to think up examples of disloyalty among friends. It is still a few notches up the emotional pole, because that is part of the attraction of role-play. Its emotional dimension, however low-key, attracts attention. That is not to deny, of course, that someone in the *non*-role play exercise, could contribute a very moving example. Indeed we shall see that *spectator* or *audience* engagement may be quite profound in all kinds of role or non-role contexts.

It is important to recognise that you have considerable control over where the emotional notch should be placed. Imagine the increase in emotional potential in B1. [let's call it B1*a*.] if you had changed your instruction slightly [let's call it B1*b*] to '*You are going to remind your friend (the listener) of an incident in the past in which you thought s/he had been disloyal by breaking a promise.*' Or, several [too many!] notches up [B1*c*], '*You are about to accuse your friend of disloyalty*'. Here we have an example of what *not* to do, unless the participants are experienced in drama. Such emotional engagement tends to lead to the worst possible kind of role play, lacking in finesse, credibility, seriousness and reflection. On the other hand, the following version may be productive even in relatively in-experienced hands:

> B1d. You set it up thus: *You are very angry with your friend who, you have learnt, has broken a promise to keep a secret. While waiting for him/her to arrive home to the apartment you share, you are deter-mined to 'have it out', but when s/he actually does arrive you cannot bring yourself to say what is on your mind.*

There is something about deliberately *withholding* expressions of anger, grief or jealousy that can bring a foundation of truthfulness to an improvisation. The awareness that the deep emotion is there but never expressed somehow makes it more 'real' for inexperienced players.

The way the *sharing* is handled is important. You can invite the class to contribute to a list of 'disloyalty' contexts by giving a label to the example you have just engaged in or you can ask them to repeat some of the stories *or* (perhaps less likely with this exercise) you could invite some pairs to *re-enact* their role-play. You would always have to ask yourself whether such re-enactment will actually in-crease the class's attention on the isssue or expand their understanding. Our hunch is that in most instances, 'reporting' or 'recounting' will be sufficient for you to move the class on to a discussion of the chosen concept. Do not use 're-enactment' or 'showing' as a time filler.

Sometimes a text may supply an impetus to discussion of a concept.

Hamlet Act 111 Scene 1

King:
And can you, by no drift of circumstance,
Get from him why he puts on this confusion,
Grating so harshly all his days of quiet
With turbulent and dangerous lunacy?

Rosencrantz:
He does confess he feels himself distracted;
But from what cause he will by no means speak.

Guildenstern:
Nor do we find him forward to be sounded;
But, with a crafty madness, keeps aloof,
When we would bring him on to some confession
Of his true state.

Queen:
Did he receive you well?

Rosencrantz:
Most like a gentleman

Guildenstern:
But with much forcing of his disposition.

One kind of role-play appropriate to the use of texts is to insert other, non-character speakers into the dialogue – and then rehearse and present it for others to consider. In this example:

B2. You split the class into groups of six, inviting them to enact the above dialogue, but to insert two kinds of commentary, preceding or immediately following each character's input. One commentator will explain how each character would *justify* this act of disloyal spying on Hamlet and the second commentator will be that of an observer, exposing the 'real' reason for the disloyalty. Thus the sequence of dialogue might be as follows:

Justifier for the King:
Here are Rosencrantz and Guildenstern. It is in order for me to set up this enquiry. I know my dear Queen is worried about him.

Observer of the King:
Does Hamlet have suspicions about how his father died?

King:
And can you, by drift of circumstances,
Get from him........*and so on.*

What form the presentation required in B2. takes depends on how comfortable the class will be with the *physical* aspect. If they are averse to enactment it is possible that they simply *read* their newly devised scripts – an unambitious way of doing it. You might like to suggest before they start rehearsing that having the King and Queen side by side on their thrones might form the basis for the action with 'Justifier' and 'Observer' speaking over the King or Queen's shoulder as appropriate. Or you could merely ask the groups to write their scripts from which you choose one which you and class co-direct: '*Where do you think the King and Queen should be?... Where should we have the 'Justifier' before s/he actually speaks? etc etc.*'

Content objectives will always dictate the choice of context and format. You may want to use text to illustrate the difference, for example, between 'disloyalty' and 'treachery'. *Othello* supplies a painful example of the latter:

Othello Act 111 Scene 111

Iago:
My noble lord, –

Othello:
What does thou say, Iago?

Iago:
Did Michael Cassio, when you woo'd my lady,
Know of your love?

Othello:
He did, from first to last: why dost though ask?

Iago:
But for the satisfaction of my thought;
No further harm.

Othello:
Why of thy thought, Iago?

Iago:
I did not think he had been acquainted with her.

Othello:
O, yes; and went between us very oft.

Iago:
Indeed!

Othello:
Indeed! ay, indeed: – discern'st though aught in that?
Is he not honest?

Iago:
Honest, my lord!

Othello:
Honest ay, honest.

Iago My lord, for aught I know.

B3. Groups of four may examine this text, with a view to putting it on its feet. Two represent the characters, simply reading the dialogue, standing at some distance away from each other, paralleled by the other two symbolically representing Othello walking into Iago's trap – perhaps as two facing figures, one with outstretched arms and a smile and the other, step by step walking into those open arms which [without actually touching] become a cage round the trapped head.

If your group are students of literature, you may want them to examine a character in a play. The initial stimulus might read like an advertisement:

B4...*Wanted: young sculptors to create statues of Shakespearean characters to inhabit a gallery of different rooms so that High School*

Students can gain some insight into the humanity of these characters. Themes of different rooms in the gallery will include Love, Revenge, Treachery, Ambition and Deception. Let us say your class choose [continuing our own example] **treachery** and select Iago as one of their treacherous characters. Their task is:

(1) to search the text [you will have laid the text out on walls or tables round the the room with all the Iago sections highlighted] for all aspects of Iago they can find. [Impress on them that they are to find the **humanity** of their character, not just 'Iago the baddie'.] and

(2) put the findings of their class together as a coherent assemblage to be **sculpted** into a meaningful representation [using people, images, written quotes from texts, voice over, commentary or even a computerised model to be accessed on CD] for a 'guest', a member of the gallery committee or an artist/craftsman.

It may be inappropriate with your group to use a text as a stimulus. You may prefer to set up an improvisation in pairs with a comparable situation.

B5. You could instruct your group to work in pairs (simultaneously throughout your work-space), characters A. and B: '*A. is malicious and is determined to damage the character of a mutual friend, C. – while pretending to be loyal to C. A. hints at something terrible C. has done. B. remains totally loyal to C. – and A. remains deceptively loyal.* In discussion, afterwards, pairs may report the kind of ploy A. used, or they may, if suitable, repeat the conversation for the benefit of the class.

Notice how restrictive in scope are the instructions for the above. Matching with A2 on Road Safety it would become:

B6. In your groups, think up a scene(s) in which someone is disloyal and get it ready to show us.

Some adolescent groups might be able to take such a task in their stride, but to what purpose? It will be far more time-consuming than, say, B5 above, without necessarily being more productive in terms of new understanding, for the freer rein of B6 may make it impossible to have a focused discussion afterwards. But if, for instance, the revised wording of B6 could be: '...*think up a scene in which someone is justified in being disloyal..*' [as perhaps Rosencrantz and Guildenstern are], this narrowing of meaning may make for more searching reflection.

Another way of improving on B6 above is, instead of tightening the *content* as above ['*think up a scene in which someone is justified in being disloyal*'] you can *tighten the audience task* and thereby, in-directly tighten the scene, so that the instruction to 'go into groups' could be as follows:

> B7... Devise a script for your scene that poses a problem for your *audience* to solve. Have one of your characters put under pressure to divulge a secret. Show the response of that character – and then invite a member of the audience to replace that actor and respond differently in a replay of the scene.

Whatever you do with B5 its success is dependent on realistic acting by the participants. One way of avoiding this is to use the Brechtian device of having the actors *narrate*:

> B7a. It might play something like this:
>
> Role of Pat, a student:
> *My friend, Sarah, had always made me promise not to tell anyone about her using drugs, but the other day our teacher called me aside.*
>
> Role of Teacher:
> *I had been worried about Sarah for some time. Last week, when I discovered her friend Pat, leaving the classroom after the other, I said 'Pat, could I have a word with you...' etc. etc.*

B7. and B7a. require a process of devising a script, rehearsing and showing in preparation for discussion of the concept. You may prefer simply to arrive speedily at the emotional heart of this kind of problem by using teacher/leader-in-role:

B8. Addressing the whole class as if they are *one* character (of Pat) or selecting one pupil to be Pat, you might begin with: *Oh, Pat could I have a word with you?... I know you are close friends with Sarah... I've been a bit concerned about her lately... her health... she doesn't seem to have been herself... Do you know... I mean, has she been all right?... etc. etc.*

In each of these you are anticipating plunging the class into a discussion of whether there are any circumstances when one is justified in being disloyal. Some teachers might make the mistake of setting up the elaborate role-play of B6. and B7., when B8. would do. And even in B8. you have a choice in respect of *physicality* and *responsibility* as discussed above. In addressing the class or just one pupil, you will decide whether it is appropriate, for that particular class, and that particular session, to just leave the role-players sitting at their desks or chairs or whether the meaning of the scene will be enhanced by actually seeing the pupil, 'Pat' waylaid by you as she was leaving the classroom.

But none of these may meet what you have in mind. If you wanted to make a greater impact; if you wanted to have an image created for your students of the awfulness or even the awesomeness of 'disloyalty' or the stronger 'betrayal' or 'treachery', then a more dramatic approach is required.

B9. You might use perhaps the most well-known example from Western literature of 'The Judas kiss'. The setting of the Garden of Gethsemane may be enacted in slow motion, for example, giving time for each witness to the kiss (Peter and John etc and the soldiers) to make a comment. If your students are religious education students, then those comments may be suitable quotes searched for by them in the biblical text.

B9a. Or you may feel that above enactment (B9.) of such a scene is too demanding on inexperienced actors, so you may introduce the idea of expressing through hands and arm gestures only. Say, four

> seated pupils representing Jesus, Judas, the soldiers and the disciples. To a carefully constructed narration they, using hands and arms only, represent the moment leading up to the kiss, the kiss and the moment after. The 'kiss' is represented, of course, merely by the touching of finger tips.

Political leaders fear disloyalty, whether it be Queen Elizabeth 1. or Margaret Thatcher:

> B10. Invite groups to create a comic mime, starting with a posed 'photograph' of Thatcher's [or a current PM's!] inner circle, [names on big labels] which gets more and more upset as the Heseltines and Howes etc move their seats away from close proximity to her.

The general advice to teachers is to avoid comedy in role-play, but, very occasionally, there is a place for the above kind of carefully rehearsed, brief presentation, in order to make a point. Notice that the comedy lies in the idea, not in actors 'being funny'. Comic performances for their own sake should be discouraged. And one should be aware of the natural 'funny man' of the group' who, unless you do something about it, will dictate where the role-play should be pitched – at a level of witty unseriousness!

One of the dangers with this kind of topic, especially where it verges on the presentation of something as sinister as deception and treachery, is that it seemingly invites students to create the evil we want them to recognise but not perpetuate. **Scripts** safely do this for you. This is why it is sometimes preferable to let the script carry the responsibility. Likewise, if you were working with younger children on a similar theme, the 'dark elements' can be introduced through **Fairy Tales**, safely avoiding children having to make up their own.

Conclusion

In this chapter, using but two topics with two contrasted age groups we have tried to give a whole range of examples which you could select from and use as, in the main, introductory role-play activities. You may find your selection leads naturally to other kinds of work or to more role-play.

Some teachers and leaders assume that in order to do the role-play you have to 'warm up' your classes with games or relaxation exercises in order to help your classes interact more easily. Your circumstances may be such that this kind of preliminary activity is necessary, but it is our experience that carefully constructed role-play or some non role-play activity related to the subject-matter carries its own way of easing a group into starting and that valuable time can be wasted in games etc. If, however, you need such 'warm ups', there are plenty of other admirable texts you can turn to for advice.

In the next chapter, we will continue to give a range of *genres*, but now bearing in mind that any example is best understood when it is seen as part of a *sequence* of activities, including other role-plays. One often chooses an exercise, aware that it is to precede a further one – and the two together make for a more meaningful experience. We shall also concentrate in the next chapter on training work with adults?'

CHAPTER TWO
ROLE-WORK FOR TRAINING ADULTS - EXAMPLES OF A RANGE OF GENRES (2)

W e continue here with our attempt to present a whole range of role-play *genres*. The principles behind some of these we will have already used in the work on Road-Safety or Disloyalty, but the format becomes very different when adults rather than pupils make up the class. As we have already pointed out at the end of the last chapter, we hope in this chapter to go beyond offering a wide selection of 'starters' to a more considered choice to be made on the basis of preparing for a sequence. We shall not, however, give a step by step recommendation for a sequence, for that would become uniquely appropriate to the particular class and the particular issue from which it may be difficult to extend to other contexts. But we will give possible extracts from a sequence, especially where the examples can show a development in complexity either of structure or subject-matter. Thus we will *indicate* a potential sequence rather than outline it. Two examples, the work on team manager-training and the training of hospital ward-managers are accounts of work that have previously been carried out.

Examples of dramatic genres available to all tutors using role-play: C. Medical students – so you want to be a doctor? D. Trainee plumbers E. Management training – Northern Gas Board and F. an account of AiM's work with hospital ward managers.

C. So you want to be a doctor?
So we have tried to offer examples of alternative starting points for opening up a theme using role-play. We have attempted to show

shades of difference in each example, starting with the least demanding and gradually increasing either in difficulty of handling the role-play or in sophistication of the subject-matter. But these two critical dimensions, one relating to the kind of role-play and the other relating to the kind of knowledge are not necessarily logically compatible, for the simplest role-play can achieve significant learning. Conversely, a great deal of time and complicated acting of dramatic scenes can lead to shallow results.

The first exercise you select may not in itself bring about the change in attitude or understanding you have in mind; you may need to select another, ...and another, so that *cumulatively* some learning can occur. In which case, it is the *sequence* of steps that becomes critical. As we said above, there is a limit to which the *spread* of alternatives may be useful, unless, of course, you could string some of them into a sequence e.g. what begins as A1 in the list of alternatives – 'Road Drill in the hall' – may be *supplemented* by the later examples dealing with the different dimensions of a road accident. Thus a sequence is created.

So, in tackling the matter of how do you introduce fresh medical trainees to the idea of being a doctor one day, we have been conscious of the need to see our examples as at least potentially part of a sequence. Indeed the examples could be envisaged as contributing to a sequential course, each step of which represents a discrete aspect of the subject-matter.

How do you start? What is the activity that the trainees will feel most comfortable with? What is the medical *topic* they are going to feel unthreatened by? How about an exercise to do with the aids they will invariably carry round with them as either doctors in practice or on the wards:

Discrete Topic: a doctor's equipment

C1a. Have a life-size drawing of a doctor -androgynous, so no details of clothes or body other than a hint of eye placement. Invite students to suggest the aids they think they will be regularly using when they

> are qualified by coming up to the body outline and placing words or drawing – e.g. stethoscope drawn from ears to hand perhaps – around the figure.

or

> C1b. Instead of one life-size drawing give each trainee a his/her own copy on which s/he can privately add words and drawings. Let them turn to small groups to compare results adding any they can think of together.

When the list for either C1a or C1b is exhausted you then invite each to write down [on own note pad] a series of statements beginning 'With a [stethoscope] I will be able to...' Make sure, as you go round, the statements are *personal*, not the impersonal, such as: 'a stethoscope checks heart and lungs'. You want the 'I' to be a 'future me'. These two examples are of incipient or implied role-play. You are inviting your trainees to visualise themselves in the future. When they have finished their list they could be invited to attempt to classify their tools as drawn and labelled. Instead of using a figure drawing of a doctor, you could have a drawing of a 'doctor's bag', inviting trainees to 'pack it' listing what they see as essentials to be carried around. Such a list could lead to a discussion of *safety rules* regarding contents and transporting. Again you will try to personalise the list, requiring each trainee at some point to speak or write of 'I will carry such and such...'

Discrete Topic: a typical day's commitments

> C2. Place a doctor's coat [outdoor or medical] plus stethoscope on back of a chair 'on stage' with its back turned towards group. A volunteer sits on chair and proceeds to record the trainees' suggestions on what a doctor is likely to have to do in a typical day.

Notice the use of the expression 'on stage' for the above undramatic exercise. This is simply to convey how the use of a simple device signing 'doctor' and the placement in an empty space of a chair *makes a doctor present.* There is no pressure on the volunteer and yet he is part of the 'theatre' that is created. Significantly all the examples so far require the trainees to give their attention to some inanimate object *outside* themselves – a large chart or pictures or a sheet of paper on which to write or the back view of a chair. These objects create a shared point of reference, making the context to be examined *safely* present. Paradoxically one often *avoids* role-play in order to start role-play!

With copies of the 'timetable' list to hand, small groups can now discuss what skills will be required of them in these different aspects of a day's work.

A discrete topic – health hazards

C3...Collect from magazines, pictures of people engaged in regular occupations – athletes, footballers, shoppers carrying bags, people lifting things, truck-drivers, craftsmen, chefs etc. These should show different ages, countries, gender and figure types. Place them on large sheets so that they can be passed round or pinned up. In *pairs* students examine them and write beside them the health hazards they can see arising from those occupations [short, and then, later, long term hazards]. When these are completed the pairs each select an occupation that interests them and take on the role of 'doctor' and 'consultant', respectively, discussing, as if the person in the photograph is the 'doctor's patient, the kind of long-term problem the doctor might spot. Each pair then repeats this consultation for the rest of the group and you will feed in on range, accuracy and scope of the medical information exchanged between the two. [Note: the tutor will not at this stage discuss their *skill* in holding such a consultation, just the knowledge involved].

Suddenly we are into role-play proper – and it shouldn't *feel* any different. The point of concentration is to be on the information they are sharing; they are not expected to be clever, pretending to be better-informed than they are. When they about to repeat it for the sake of the rest of the class, you will emphasise that fellow trainees are to examine the quality of the *information*. This could be a key moment in your use of role-play and any mishandling by participants showing off or being funny or witty must be nipped in the bud immediately – or the whole purpose of the exercise becomes distorted – for ever! It is simply a demonstration of their thinking through the topic for others to consider and build upon. Set up properly you will move into the low-key exercise almost imperceptibly, so that they are barely aware that role-play has started.

Now we are shifting the angle of the topic, away from the doctor as an individual to **community** practice. The contextual signs are many and complex, for they embrace the whole *ambience* of a medical centre: all the administrative comings and goings, all the indications of this as a caring place, plus the particular style and function of each separate surgery.

A discrete topic – designing a medical centre and surgery

C4. Hand out to each trainee a sheet showing a simple architectural plan [architect's logo at top] of a building with door/window placements and dimensions indicated. You will now switch to being in role as a representative of the architect's firm: '*I appreciate you are busy people, but it is important that essential matters are hammered out now...etc etc.*' and you go on to say your brief at this stage is to know about the placing of permanent fittings which will need to be incorporated into this new Health Centre., starting with private consulting rooms. '*So, what do you advise us about plumbing, heating, lighting, computing, waste disposal design of reception area etc...?*'

'Doctors' consider in pairs; the 'architect' goes round taking notes. When the pairs have conferred you hold a public discussion – your 'colleague from the firm' acting as scribe with overhead projector or flip-chart, so that the suggestions are 'made public'. [The 'architect' leaves and *you* can return to hold an in depth discussion of their suggestions for health clinic designs in an ideal world!

This is the first example we have included in this 'medical' section of using the 'meeting' convention where you are required to lead your class into their 'collective' task by playing a simple 'chair' role. There are a number of Do's and Don'ts that might be helpful here.

1. Make sure you prepare your group for the convention. Don't suddenly start 'being an architect' or it will seem threatening or gimmicky. You might say *'When I've given out these sheets... as a way of thinking ourselves into the problem of necessities... I'll be a visiting architect...'*. As you say this your class are glimpsing the letter-heading on the sheets you are handing out.

2. Do use visual signals, giving some *authenticity* to the occasion – brief-case; letter heading. Try to use appropriate language style, but *no more!* You are not creating a character or performing a role to impress.

3. Nor should you make demands on your group to behave any differently than usual. What you are asking of them is to think themselves into the problem and to try to express their ideas in public terms that would be meaningful to someone from another profession – in this case, architecture. It is this having to reshape their thinking into an appropriate form of communication that tends to give status to the problem and to sharpen thinking.

4. Notice that you hover 'taking notes' as they talk quietly in pairs. This must not be a pose; you must genuinely be interested in what they are coming up with. Anything less will ring untrue. What you are generating is an overlap between actuality and fiction. Your trainees must simply be absorbed in their task, *released* from playing in a fiction to do with being doctors called away from their work to meet an architect. And yet, *at the edge of their consciousness*, you are perpetuating that fiction, a gentle reminder, no more, that they are part of it and will be resuming their roles in it.

5. When they give their suggestions you now put some pressure on them by your professional manner to be back in the fiction to which they have some responsibility.

And now, moving away from a consideration of the whole clinic to the particular surgery within it:

C4a An empty architect's design [name of community clinic heading] for a typical doctor's surgery are given to each trainee whose name is to be written at the top. Windows, doors, telephone/power/computer points and water source plus dimensions are indicated. 'Doctors' are asked by you now in role as 'Practice manager' of this new building how they would like to arrange their surgeries: furniture, lighting, position of computer, 'privacy' curtain and their colour preferences. Emphasise need for accuracy, as though instructing delivery personnel where to place each item.

The rooms can then be discussed in small groups. In leading the discussion, you now switch your role to that of 'senior partner'. 'Doctor partners' can amend their plans if they hear a better idea expressed.

The above is not just an exercise in planning a room; it also, if you play your role with some subtlety, opens up the critical process of **consultation**. Notice that you are required to play two roles, the 'practice manager' and the 'senior partner', offering two different perspectives on restarting work in a new building.

Now let us turn to a central consultation issue in the medical world:

Discrete topic – the doctor/ patient relationship

C5...a representation of a patient visiting her/his doctor. Using copies of the same pictures [without any written health hazards] in pairs one trainee represents the person in the picture and presents a selected problem to the 'doctor' [the other partner]. These consultations, touching on doctor/patient interaction in respect of diagnosis, perhaps bringing out a possible mismatch between a patient's view of the occupational problem and the doctor's wider perception, are then repeated for the whole group to consider.

Once again, these interactions are offered in the spirit of 'pooling ideas', not being clever about information – and certainly not acting! It is simply one group of people putting forward or demonstrating an idea for another group of people to consider.

and

C6...Display a *different* set of magazine pictures, this time of different kinds of persons rather than their activities, showing something of age, kind of personality, life-style, clothes style etc, and in pairs they plan (a) some aspect of the observed personality that might itself be a problem in a first consultancy [either at patient's home or in surgery], such as diffidence, reserve, fear, exaggeration tendencies, embarrassment, denial etc and (b) what the medical problem is [not an obvious one this time – it could be a sleep problem or worry or a vague pain. The trainees must predecide these two aspects, for the exercise has nothing to do with sudden surprises or catching someone out. They try out the roles and then repeat them for the others. This time the focus of discussion is solely on quality of patient/doctor contact.

and

C7. You will prepare two envelopes for each pair, one containing authentic forms which a GP might receive from a hospital showing results of tests and diagnoses plus any recommended follow up treatment; the other containing a picture [as C6 above] of a person, showing age, sex, race and something of personality and background information about previous ailment and the kind of test carried out by laboratory. It might read as:

> *damaged leg with garden fork*
> *wound not healing*
> *swab taken and analysed in laboratory*
> *now visiting your own doctor for results of test*

Whereas the 'doctor's' instructions read:

> *There is some evidence of infection in the leg wound*
> *It will require an antibiotic*
> *and frequent attendance at the clinic for dressings*
> *Check: that the patient understands the need for strict*
cleanliness
> *............that the patient understands timing of tablets at*
> *regular intervals*
> *............that the patient understands the wound will not*
> *heal swiftly.*

Each pair will decide their respective roles of doctor and patient and open the appropriate envelope – without the other seeing its contents.

> While they ponder on the implications of their respective pieces of information each pair 'finds a space' and 'sets' the room, indicating position of door, furniture etc. Without any discussion each pair of partners tries out the consultation.

The trainees (all at the same time throughout your work-space) will try this at least three times. The exercise burdens each role-player with an imposed agenda, so the initial interaction should simply be used to feel at ease with the information. Make sure you set it up in a semi-casual way that allows them to 'play' with the material. You might say: *'We're going to do this more than once. Don't worry this first time if you stumble over the information; you'll need time to absorb it all – but, have a go!'* For their second run-through, warn them that you will interrupt at some point, requiring them to break off in order to tell each other at which points so far there was real communication between doctor and patient. When they have finished the exercise they will again reaffirm where they felt the strengths of their consultation lay.

The importance of this task of identifying their own skills cannot be overemphasised. Do not be tempted to let them 'wallow' in charades! Here we have a typical, complex, interview situation in which each side carries its own agenda and in which it is so easy to deceive oneself into thinking communication is taking place. Trainees will only learn about their skills in such a context if due attention is given to them. Thus, before showing their interview to other members of the class, you will require them to make a list of what they see as its effective moments, a list which is then read to the class before the partners demonstrate it to them. In turn, the members of the audience, their note-books to hand, write down when they recognise those moments of strength.

Incidentally, because some of the examples given out to the partners could have very grave implications – such as identification of cancer – it could be a 'relative' or 'close friend', rather than the 'patient' as the interviewee, so that the role-player is saved from bad news highly personalised.

The most elusive discrete topic: 'reading' the patient

So far, in considering setting up the use of role to put trainees in touch with constituent aspects of being a doctor, we have asked them to consider a sequence of targets such as contents of a doctor's bag, the recognition of occupational hazards, the recognition that the design of a health centre and its surgeries sends a message to patients, the recognition that doctor and patient have their separate agendas.

Now it is one thing to know that doctor and patient carry different agendas, but it is entirely another matter for a young doctor to be able to 'read' where a patient is coming from and additionally be able to intuit how the patient is 'reading' the doctor. It could be that you would like your trainees to at least have some insight into their likely skill in 'reading' from the very beginning of their course. The exercises that follow will perhaps allow the trainees a glimpse of something they need to develop in themselves through practice.

Behind each exercise is the question: **When you listen to a patient's 'story', what do you 'see'? What do you 'stand up' in your mind?**

To test themselves on their ability to 'stand up images in their minds', we suggest you use a medical story from literature. The reason for this choice of stimulus is twofold. It carries the authenticity of a 'real case' and it is dense with images.

C8...Have a very short story read [a good tape-recording of a reading of a well-written 'medical' anecdote would guarantee capturing your class's attention e.g. pp 18-19 of Richard Selzer's *Confessions of a knife: meditations on the Art of Surgery* – see below] and ask each trainee, after one or two hearings, to list and then share with a neighbour the images he 'saw' from just one reading. You write up on large sheets any interesting differences in kinds of images recalled.

You will appreciate that once more we appear to have abandoned role-play, but in a way, when we 'read' a social situation and turn it over in our heads to make it accessible to ourselves, we are engaged in a kind of mental role-play. Whatever we call it, it is a necessary process that all doctors have to go through almost daily. They have to find their own 'version' of someone else's 'version'. Now in 'real life' a doctor hears a patient's story and translates it first into his own mental imagery and then into professional advice. The above exercise merely offers a parallel of finding mental and then written images of a piece of fiction. What may be illuminating to your trainees is that we all tend to notice different things, that our monitoring is selective. From discussing their written materials in groups it should be possible to recognise distinct and positive areas which have not occurred to individuals.

Now the medical anecdote referred to above by the remarkable literary surgeon, Richard Selzer[1]:

What is to one man a coincidence is to another a miracle. It was one or the other of these I saw last spring. While the rest of nature was in flux, Joe Riker remained obstinate through the change of the seasons. 'No operation,' said Joe. 'I don't want no operation'...

Joe Riker is a short-order cook in a diner where I sometimes drink coffee. Each week for six months he had paid a visit to my office, carrying his affliction like a pet mouse under his hat. Every Thursday at 4'o'clock he would sit on my examining table, lift the fedora from his head, and bend forward to show me the hole. Joe Riker's hole was as big as his mouth. You could have dropped a plum in it. Gouged from the tonsured top of his head was a mucky puddle whose meaty heaped edge rose above the normal scalp about it. There was no mistaking the announcement from this rampart.

The cancer had chewed through Joe's scalp, munched his skull, then opened the membranes underneath – the dura mater, the pia mater, the arachnoid until it had laid bare the short-order cook's brain, pink and gray, and pulsating so that with each beat a little pool of cerebral fluid quivered. Now and then a drop would manage the rim to run across his balding head, and Joe would reach one burry hand up to wipe it away, with the heel of his thumb, the way such a man would wipe away a tear.

I would gaze then upon Joe Riker and marvel. How dignified he was, as though that tumor, gnawing him, denuding his very brain, had given him a grace that a lifetime of good health had not bestowed.

'Joe', I say, 'let's get rid of it. Cut out the bad part, put in a metal plate, and you're cured.' And I wait.

'No operation,' says Joe. I try again.

'What do you mean, 'no operation'? you're going to get meningitis. Any day now. And die. That thing is going to get to your brain.'

I think of it devouring the man's dreams and memories. I wonder what they are. The surgeon knows all the parts of the brain, but he does not know his patient's dreams and memories. And for a moment I am tempted... to take the man's head in my hands, hold it to my ear, and listen. But his dreams are none of my business. It is his flesh that matters.

'No operation,' says Joe.

'You give me a headache,' I say. And we smile, not because the joke is funny any more, but because we've got something between us, like a secret.

'Same time next week?' Joe asks. I wash out the wound with peroxide and apply a dressing. He lowers the fedora over it.

'Yes, I say, 'same time.' And the next week he comes again.

and

C8a Now, as if preparing to enact the scene as described in the anecdote, ask your class, in pairs, (working simultaneously throughout the work-space) to become the 'director' of the scene and 'the model of one of the characters in the story', respectively. The 'director' will instruct the 'model' on the features of the character that he wants brought out in a selected piece of behaviour from the anecdote. For instance (using the Selzer story), the 'director' might say to partner:

'When you come into the surgery we need to know that you are confident, you've been here often, you know where the doctor will want you to sit and even what he will say – and you will keep your hat on. So...lets try that' And the partner will now enact that entry into the surgery and then receive feedback from the 'director' who will try to describe what he could 'read' from gestures, tone of voice, appearance etc, as though the director was preparing a TV presentation.

The whole scene is gone through, the emphasis is to capture the spirit of the patient's handling of the problem. So all details of the account are compounded into the style of the patient's behaviour – repetitive weekly visit, stubborn refusal to have surgery, clothing of a short-order cook, fedora, courtesy, patience, and gesture of wiping away the escaping fluid.

Functions are then reversed, the second partner now becoming 'director' to the 'model of the doctor', instructing partner on the doctor's respect and fearing for the patient, his attempt at persuading and his yielding with the amazing 'you give me a head-ache', the washing and binding.

> They should not show work to the rest of the group. Each pair, using the same anecdote, will have found its own slow and perhaps tedious way into 'where each is coming from'.

These demonstrations are not a competition – they are an exercise in

> C8b...Working faster now, having heard a second anecdote you've chosen from medical literature , they will in pairs go through the two-way director's process, this time with a view to demonstrating to the others. It will not, however, be a straightforward enactment, but rather an actor/narrative, so that one partner might explain as s/he does the actions: '*My director thought that this patient would knock like this and enter like this and that I should say....*' and the other partner, in turn, *narrates* what *his/her* director has instructed.
>
> Other pairs will volunteer and demonstrate how they had envisioned it and so on....

proving to oneself that one can carry conceptions about interaction into active behaving and explaining of their perspectives. Literature is an essential ingredient because it provides parameters to permit engagement with depth and probing. It also widens your trainees' experience of encounters especially when they stretch beyond the ones they can invent for themselves from their own experience.

An overview topic – looking beyond the routine

> C9 Your class are going to work in small groups, devising a written script that will be 'put on its feet' for the rest of the class. The 'frame' is that you, in your role as producer, have been asked to direct a TV series for 6th formers to give them an idea whether a career in medicine attracts them. '*The script-writers have already gone to work on the scripts – I have them here*' You address your class as medical experts called in to advise on what explanations [voice over] need to accompany the performance of the text, so that the young viewers

understand the implications of any routine actions included. For instance, if there was a hand-washing action as part of a consultation, a voice-over might elaborate for the viewer by explaining *how many times a day hand-washing occurs; how there is a pattern to doing it thoroughly, quickly; that it becomes second nature and automatic.*

You give a different script out to each group who prepare to demonstrate it to the others, adding whatever explanatory narrative they think would be useful. The audience listen, carefully checking whether the information is clear and precise – and the kind of thing to interest pre-University students.

Typically, a script might read as follows:

Scene: Waiting area B at hospital outpatients' department. patient is seated reading a book. Nurse opens a door and calls patient's name. Patient closes book, takes off glasses, collects belongings, rises and follows nurse into consulting room.

Surgeon is standing – in ordinary suit – with a colleague. S/he has the consulting file and notes. Comes forward, greets patient, introduces colleague:

'*Well, we now have the results of your examination.....and I can confirm that there are some cancer cells – early stages... and I think we should deal with this as soon as convenient to yourself....*'...and the script develops the caring support of the three professionals.

D. Training apprentices

This section sets out to help trainers in industry, commerce and public services to use role-play in their own courses, at whatever level of training is required, whether it be beginner shop assistants or top executives. The *principles* guiding choice of role-play apply to all levels.

The authors of this book do not claim to have knowledge of the kind of work that the role-play will often refer to, for it is not the skill in the craft or technical knowledge that role-play aims to improve. Role-play comes into its own when dealing with those human and social elements that accompany the carrying out of the craft so that the same principles of role-play can apply across a wide range of jobs.

Supposing we were to give an illustration in the role work of, say, a hotel chef baking a birthday cake; it matters not whether we know how to bake a cake [one of us does, the other doesn't!], for the role-play will be exposing aspects such as 'how do you cope with pressures of time', 'organisation of kitchen', 'allocation of staff duties', 'customer complaints' etc. – those points in the working day when matters beyond the chef's skill itself can go wrong or be improved.

Now in order to suggest how role play might be set up by *your* trainers, we in this text would make references to aspects of a chef's work, *as though we know all about it*. Well we don't! It is merely convenient to suggest an exercise without continually qualifying it with remarks such as '*If this is the kind of thing you do in your work...*'. However, what is most important to understand, is that if we were to find ourselves employed by your chef-training scheme to carry out the kind of role-play we are suggesting on one of your courses, we would need to visit you and find out about the *particular* human/social problems of the work. It is not enough for the tutor conducting the role-play to have some vague ideas about possible problems. S/he would need advice on particular issues and on the reality of the particular working conditions. We shall towards the end of this chapter be giving an illustration of the work done by **Action in Management**[2], a Co. Durham firm of consultants trainers who use drama as a way of improving management skills. Before they work with a particular firm, they visit the site, factory or premises, meeting up with their clients in order to familiarise themselves with current management problems. And we are assuming in writing this text that whoever attempts to use the ideas will *know* the nature of the work *from the inside* and will therefore be in a position to *adapt* our exercises to those circumstances.

We have not in fact chosen the 'chef' context for illustrating principles, but the more common one of an employee/craftsman dealing with customers in their own home. This is a good example of 'common sense' procedures – working tactfully (no loud radios, no smoking, no pressure to get 'go ahead'), working tidily, clearing up, protecting property – carpets, furniture when carrying things, correct identification of self and purpose, stacking vans safely, form filling, signatures from householders and so on.

The above could fit most craftspersons' visits to private homes, but the particular example we have in mind is that of gas-fitters and we have written our suggestions from the point of view of 'senior' gas staff responsible for building 'customer' skills in less experienced employees e.g. gas fitter apprentices. How might you senior staff use role-play to prepare apprentices for this domestic work?

Let us imagine you starting off a course. What is going to guide you to choice of exercise? You're certainly not going to ask them to act. Talking may not be a strong point. In the circumstances of finding themselves 'on a course!', they may not want to *do* anything. Getting off their chairs may be just too much. Okay, try *using* their chairs and, further, let the first exercise be limited to following routine instructions:

> D1 Supposing you say to your group as (perhaps as you sit in a circle with them) '*This chair is my driving seat...here's my bag of tools* [real or something representing it] *and I've got my identification card... and a signature form... I'm just driving along the street, looking for the right number. Between me switching off the engine and going to the front door, there's an order of doing things. Okay, I'll do it: Break... switch off the engine... check I've got identification... check form for signature... write down time of arrival... put pen back... get out of vehicle... pick up tool bag... lock van... put the key in...'* Now ask them to do it on their chairs as you say it: '*Break... switch off engine etc...'* Now ask them to repeat the sequence while you remain silent.

They have not been required to 'act' being a gas-fitter. It has been a memory exercise, their success with which you ask them to evaluate. [Other related matters to do with care in parking could arise out of this, so that, for instance, checking in mirror before opening the van door could be suggested and inserted into a revised sequence]. So you could find yourself adding:

> D1a '*Let's just check where we're up to now... John, could you do it for us?... the full sequence... to see if we've got it right... say what you're doing as you do it.'* And then others, now speak the sequence aloud – as you did in your first example

And you've planted the idea of talking aloud as an accompaniment to the exercise. At first you demonstrated this commentary and then got one other to do it and then the whole group simultaneously. This is a first step in commenting on what one is doing as one does it. It is a key convention in that it both suspends any possibility of believing that one is acting and is an introduction to self-spectatorship. For a final form of reflection the group could create a document, a 'master' memoir for future trainees.

The above exercises are examples of rigid drill. Most role-play is to do with forms of interaction that cannot be drilled. So you are mostly training for much more open contexts. However common the procedure, ultimately the interaction will be idiosyncratically contingent. The shop assistant may be familiar with the polite but firm routine for dealing with complaining customers but no two interactions will be exactly alike. Thus most role-play practice must allow for this degree of unpredictability without stretching its believability.

In giving your trainees practice in entering customers' houses, the examples you choose should be selected with care. Although it is conceivable that a gas employee arrive just when a man and wife are throwing things at each other or when a seductive customer opens the door, such contexts are 'over the top' from the point of view of seriously approached role-play. Indeed, it is one of the problems of role-play that participants will often go for the outrageous in order to entertain – and thus *avoid* taking it seriously. You will have to set a limit to the scope of the examples. One might include having a *child* open the door, an occurrence that is not uncommon in real life but could be destructive of the work if introduced too early in the role-play. So your solution may be to start with 'straightforward' examples – whatever 'straightforward' means in the context of humankind! – and then move on to less typical ones such as dealing with a child.

Perhaps show a range of pictures of people. Give the class time to browse through them and consider them as possible houseowners who are about to open the front door to the gas fitter:

D2. Invite trainees to turn to the person they're sitting next to and between you select from the pictures which one is going to 'open *the door to you*'. and then you continue with: '*You are going to go over with your partner the kind of conversation you and the chosen houseowner might have... but first... I'll just do an example... Ken, can you be my partner for a minute... D'you want to be the fitter or the houseowner?... Okay... I'm ringing the bell then and I wait what seems ages, but isn't really... and the door is opened by this chap* [you wave the picture for others to see]...*now what do you see Ken?... Start with 'I'm opening the door...'* ... and you hope the one you have chosen, Ken, is comfortable enough to proceed with 'I see the gas fitter' or 'I see a stranger' etc and then you can take your turn with '*I get out my identification card* [minimum gesture] *and say ...*' When you have gone through a sample interaction you invite comments and then '*Try it with your partner...*'. And they all have a go.

This seemingly simple exercise can teach us a lot about the do's and don'ts of role-play. Traditionally, the tutor would have invited volunteers from his/her class to step out to the front and **improvise** a fitter/houseowner scene. This causes embarrassment and invites laughter at someone's expense. Note what we have built in to the exercise:

1. There is no 'front of class'. You are all, including the tutor, in a circle of chairs.

2. You have 'modelled' the exercise, that is, (a) voluntarily allowed yourself to be stared at first (b) adopted a style of talking as you set it up that suggests this is 'no big deal'. '*Okay... I'm ringing the bell...*'. This is sufficiently casual – and your 'ringing the bell' gesture will be fittingly token – (c) demonstrated how to talk about what you are doing either before or as you do it and (d) shown by your reaction to their comments that your interest in what they have to say is far from casual: you treat their remarks with huge respect.

3. When your class do it they are all going to be doing it at the same time – against a hub-bub of talking.

4. They do it sitting down, so that they've hardly changed their physical position, just 'turned to a neighbour'. Again, 'no big deal'.

5. There is still the opportunity for one or more couples to redo theirs so that they can make some point they want to share with the group. [Notice that 'can make some point' – it has nothing to do with 'showing a scene' – at this stage of your course.]

The talking aloud, describing what you are doing and thinking as it happens fulfils two objectives. It removes any misunderstanding that this is acting, that they have to make it 'seem like real', but it also, and more importantly as a preparation for future work, establishes the idea of self-spectatorship as a key element in role-play. And, **it is because they are sitting down,** that talking aloud in this way seems feasible. If you had simply asked them to simulate 'approaching a front door', 'ringing the bell', 'saying who you are' etc. without this preliminary 'sitting down' experience, they would find 'talking aloud' absurdly unrealistic at a time when they are struggling to be realistic. Having done this kind of commentary 'sitting down', it will then not seem illogical to them to continue to do it should they be ready to '*walk*' through the exercise.

Thus there may be two extensions of D2 above. You may find they are now ready to get on their feet to do subsequent exercises and they may also become inventive about more problematic examples of house-owner behaviour – the person opening the door cannot hear, or needs glasses to read identification card, or has left a saucepan boiling over or wants to give the fitter a drink of tea *before* any work is done. It is in such examples that it is most important that both players continue to talk aloud about their thoughts, otherwise it becomes no more than mild entertainment. You want it to be 'a looking *into*', not 'a looking *at*'.

More searching role-play

Let us now look at a tricky kind of fitter/customer interaction – and an ever trickier kind of role-play! For now the role-play is going to require the very kind of naturalism we have been avoiding.

Let's consider those occasions when the fitter is required to *instruct* about safety regulations [perhaps unpalatable to the owner] or *teach* the use of an appliance that the owner does not understand.

We need in this connection to look at the notions of 'signing' and 'reading'. They will be discussed in detail later in the book, but it is important to explain it briefly here in order to expand the above and subsequent exercises. In all social contexts we all send out messages or signs, verbal and non-verbal, sometimes intentionally and at other times without realising it. We cannot *not* sign! Sometimes the verbal and the non-verbal signs contradict each other: 'What a lovely party', I say as I smother a yawn, is a crude example! Now any gas fitter/customer interaction is about 'reading signs'. The fitter must 'read' whether the houseowner is anxious about him being there; the house-owner must be helped to feel less concerned as he 'reads' the fitter. So there could be a third extension to Exercise D2. Whereas the self-commentary had been concerned with 'What I am doing?', those scenes could be replayed to include 'What I am **reading**?'. But you as tutor need to demonstrate this first. They need *you* to play out an interaction focusing on what you are 'reading' in your partner's responses – and you will need to demonstrate both fitter's and owner's 'thinking aloud'. Otherwise they will not necessarily understand the kind of thing you want them to look for.

Thus, so far in this sequence of role-play *genres*, we have moved from (1) a relatively casual 'conversational' representation of introductory interaction by players sitting in pairs, describing aloud the actions involved but not actually doing them, through (2) getting the same kind of exercise 'on its feet', still 'thinking aloud' about the actions, to (3) concentrating on 'reading signs' in their thinking aloud.

But you may feel, with some justification, that the very act of 'thinking aloud' about the signs militates against the players properly adopting the very behaviour you want them to 'read', that what we need is 'naturalistic' acting, a genre of role-play we have been avoiding at all costs. Yet the self commentary accompanying any action or dialogue takes the action out of existential time; it hovers between past and future and merely **indicates** the present. You may feel that for an exercise that is closely linked with natural, non-verbal signals, the participants need to experience the sense of 'it is happening now', so that the responses they register can occur in 'now time' and not in this hybrid indicator of the present. Without having to comment, their natural reactions in the situation have a better chance of emerging. Thus we are back to 'improvisation' with all its pitfalls for inexperienced players. For we are asking them to do what actors do well – play out a scene authentically.

A professional company such as *Action in Management* solves this problem by having on their staff a group of actors who can make any kind of action seem 'real', as we shall see at the end of this chapter. But there is a way of getting your trainees to attempt this kind of improvisation – **by placing the burden of responsibilities on the observers**. You will make it quite clear that the effectiveness of this more sophisticated form of exercise will depend on whether the *observers* are up to the mark. You are going to ask them to function as **directors** whose aim is to discover the most positive forms of signalling, within the kind of tricky but typical interaction we describe below.

D3. Divide your class into groups of three, two players and one 'director'. You ask the directors to give out the cards to their two players – one 'fitter' and one 'houseowner' instruction card. The fitter's might read:

Essential you point out that under the new regulations the customer's garage should have a proper gas vent

You have completed the boiler inspection, but have to tell him/her this before you can leave.

The customer's card reads:

The fitter has just completed the annual inspection of your boiler kept in the garage, but before he can leave, he has to warn you about a new regulation. You don't want to hear this.

Simultaneously with other groups the three people try out (in 'real' action now) the interaction required, the 'director' guiding his players towards the 'positive signing' s/he has in mind. But this time they will not provide a commentary of what they are doing. They will play it 'straight'.

When the groups have worked out what they want to do, each observer in turn explains to the rest of the group what s/he is aiming at – and uses the players, in replaying the scene for the others to watch, to bring out the signing the 'director' wants. The audience will note down their observations as the scene is played. Finally, the whole group may make its own list of 'positive signing'.

This is the first example we have included in this section of trainees using naturalistic behaviour to show the rest of the group. It is such a beguiling *genre* that attention to signing may become suspended. It is very difficult for any kind of audience to analyse behaviour, for it is deeply embedded in our culture that when we watch a dramatic presentation we look for 'what is going to happen next', so that asking an audience to do anything else goes against its natural impulse. This is why it is essential that the 'director' focuses the audience's attention on signing behaviour before the scene starts and that the audience have their notebooks at hand. The 'director' may even interrupt the flow of the scene by asking the players at key points to stop and replay certain 'signings'. S/he will of course have warned the players that s/he might do this, and indeed will have agreed what signal for stopping the scene could be satisfactory – yelling STOP! may not be the best!

This is the most difficult form of improvisation to handle, but if you have built it up gradually through modelling, sitting, commentating and directing, then you may be surprised how the confidence of your group has been built up. They may reach the point where they could engage in what is popularly called 'Forum Theatre', in which the audience can interrupt and either *point out* an alternative signing or actually take the place of a player to *demonstrate* that alternative. This is a very advanced technique. It may be safe to assume that your trainees are not going to be ready for it. There are plenty of other ways, as we have seen above.

Onto safer ground now, let us remind ourselves that it is not just adapting to the house-owner that is required of the fitter, but also adapting to the *house!* There are responsibilities arising in the house itself. Let's assume it's a fairly big job for a trainee to tackle cutting a pipe connected to an existing appliance such as a gas fire or cooker:

D4. Discuss with group what the *technical* procedures are to be. Having agreed these, ask one pair to demonstrate them, showing how the work might be divided between the two of them. They will handle the real tools but just imagine the appliance and pipes etc. You now ask the same pair to repeat the exercise, but this time you give them a plan of a room, showing position of the appliance in relation to other furniture [just labelled shapes] and items such as polished side-tables, delicate ornaments, light-coloured immovable carpeting and a heavy plant pot stand just where they would have knelt down to the appliance. Further 'awkward' plans can be given out to other pairs who have to work out and demonstrate matters such as where do they place their toolbag, where do they put down tools not in use, do they ask for newspapers for the floor, do they offer to move the furniture that will be in the way, what do they do about cleaning up afterwards? etc etc.

E. Training managers – creating a metaphor

We are now moving into a different conception of role-play. In the above 'apprentices' section the role-play set out to bring specific interactional problems to the attention of the trainees so that they could anticipate them and have some skills to draw on when they are actually 'on the job'. In the role-play examples that follow the focus is on something much less tangible: its purpose is to be part of a grooming of a group of selected managers to understand team behaviour. The course they are on will assist them to discover their strengths and weaknesses in a team context. And role-play will contribute to this in a special way.

It will be seen that this type of role-play must be built layer by layer, so that participants have time to become immersed and committed to success. The role-play will be a mirror in which they may watch themselves and see how they 'grow' during the exercise. It is difficult to understand the examples below without appreciating the *particular* context they were originally devised for. An overarching metaphor has to be chosen by the leader. The metaphor acts as a 'thin screen' providing a parallel with the managers' own work. The metaphor can only be meaningful to the managers if they can con-tinually see through its 'screen' to their own situation and likewise it can only be meaningful to readers of this text if they know what is being paralleled.

It is therefore necessary for you to appreciate that the course in this particular case was set up by Northern Gas at a time when a complete transformation was to occur in the source of domestic gas supply – the new source of gas was to be from the North Sea. A group of managers were to be creamed off for taking on a three-fold responsibility in respect of (1) transporting safely (2) training workers and users and (3) avoiding exploitation, waste and theft. Thus these special staff were to be faced with transporting a product from an unfamiliar environment, teaching others who might be hostile to understand what needed to be done, and anticipating problems – all to be done with urgency. The task required them to *cooperate* in assessing, *cooperate* in rethinking, *cooperate* in planning the teaching of others and cooperate in avoidance plans. Whatever they did hitherto in the industry was to be laid on one side for this joint consultation and planning task – the industry was virtually in a crisis. The question for Northern Gas was 'Which of our managers has the capacity for this degree of commitment and imaginative cooperation?' – and can role-play *teach* them to examine themselves and improve themselves as 'cooperators'.

The **metaphor**: they were to be a team of experts to be hired by a Third World island [fictitious name of Gongua – huge coal source recently discovered near the coast] to help take the first step towards its newly realised economic potential by advising on (1) the development of an infrastructure whereby resources can be transported between locations (2) raising the level of education and (3) introducing a relevant legal framework.

Thus the parallel between the manager's career task and the fictitious task is clear – within the fiction they are going to be required to cooperate in assessing, rethinking, in planning to teach others and in anticipating problems. The operative theme, dominating career and fiction, is to be **team cooperation** – under the pressure of deadlines!

How to conduct the metaphoric task

From the beginning they must trust it. From the beginning they must know that it is really about themselves and their team skills. Only as it develops will they fully appreciate that the 'thin screen' is indeed very thin. Only as it develops will they know what it is like to gain sufficient insight into the way they operate in groups to make positive change – in a safe, no-penalty, fictitious zone. So they can make mistakes and learn from them. It only takes this new knowledge about themselves to open their eyes just once or twice in the early stages of the project and commitment to the project increases threefold. A kind of cautious zeal [the contradiction of terms is deliberate] overtakes the group as they see themselves overcoming cooperative barriers.

You can make a contract with them before you start that the fiction may contain the unexpected (just as in their own work) but it will sustain a logical coherence – you are not going to move the goals posts. They can trust it to give it their fullest commitment. Less than this and it will fail to illumine how they operate in groups when under pressure of time.

The *precise* features of what is meant by team cooperation

You need to be aware of these and base individual episodes on them. The project will be a slow accumulation over several sessions and will contain many different kinds of episodes having particular biases, testing different aspects of team cooperation without having recourse to a higher dictat. You will need to make sure all aspects are covered. In the Northern Gas work they were seen as:

1. Grasping a complex situation quickly

2. Deciding to take the plunge and join the task

3. Perceiving difficulties/opportunities in advance

4. Looking for congruence in team members' ideas

5. Dealing with possible colleague problems

6. Creating a scheme as a team

7. Communicating ideas to upper management

8. Collecting data

9. Final preparations

10. Dealing with setbacks

11. Final decision to continue or drop the team project

Preparation

1. You will provide each member of the group with a journal. Pages fairly small, private by implication, but could be shared (loaned, read out aloud from, become a library archive for other teams) if people ever wish to use them more publicly. From the beginning of the whole exercise you will establish that a record be kept of perceptions, changes of thinking, references to negative or positive inputs.

and

2. The objects that are going to give authenticity to the enterprise. (1) An introductory letter giving them clues about the nature of the job. It must be a professional letter to satisfy professional people – but not go into sufficient detail, indeed it can be deliberately ambiguous, so that questions can hang in the air. (2) A large map – large enough for the whole group to stand round. It must contain evidence of terrain (especially elevations), collections of population (sparse and dense), compass orientation, meandering roads, sparse tracks, farmland, forest. A neglected railway line, leading to no particular point of use; an unused canal and other waterways. This preparation is critical – appearance of map must stand up to a certain degree of believability, *but it must signal that it is made for fictional, yet believable use.* A genuine map with a name change is a cheat – it does not preserve the internal coherence of the role work.

It is not necessary that the leader plan *all* the subsequent role-play sessions before the sequence can begin – in fact it can be a disadvantage because there is a danger that useful opportunities may occur which are missed because the leader is bound up with what s/he 'knows' is going to happen next.

Some examples of episodes

It would not be possible here to give a full account of the whole project. What we have done is to select a few examples to give you an idea of the *kind* of role-play that could be employed. Let us begin with the opening episode, related to (1) above.

Grasping a situation quickly

E1. In role as 'secretary to the Ambassador of Gongua' you thank the team for coming, arriving on time and for considering the Gonguan government's request for technical advice. You pass round copies, showing more detail [but incomplete] of what is required, of a letter from the Ambassador. You give them time to read the letter and await their reactions, ready to answer questions – within your limited knowledge your role has of the enterprise.

Their questions should lead to your showing them the map of Gongua, which in turn leads you to confess that *'Gentlemen, I have to inform you that our transport and education systems are at present not entirely adequate, though we are negotiating a loan from the world bank and anticipate no problems there... You should understand, gentlemen, that our people are proud and independent and previous administrations have not seen their way to establishing a formal system of law, leaving authority to be invested in tribal domains... But now we have discovered rich seams of brown coal at the coast line... if developed and exported wisely... it would bring Gongua into the present century... we need technical assistance and mature advice... We ask: is this viable regarding transport, education and relevant law? My ambassador – and, of course, your enterprise which has loaned your services to us – need to know whether this is viable? Can you assess difficulties, foresee possibilities and indicate an approach to what really is a huge, new opportunity?...etc. etc.'*

The above dialogue is intended to be interactional rather than a monologue as printed here and it can be accompanied by reference to the map. You are looking for two opportunities (1) to set the task for the next meeting – the group should divide into three teams each with a different responsibility [transport, education, regulations] to present a draft plan at the next meeting and (2) look for the right moment to come out of role to establish 'self-examination' and 'group examination', tasks which will at this stage be conducted privately into their journals. You will not be sure whether setting the task for 'the next meeting' will be done in or out of role – it depends how it goes.

Not only are you looking for when to come out of role, but you must do it in a way that seems perfectly natural – a congratulatory smile and a change in quality of voice you use as you say something like... '*Can I interrupt and be myself for a minute?...*'

This is the crucial part of the first 'episode', for you will emphasise the need for rigour in the observation of themselves and what happened to them as a group. How far did they get with achieving 'a speedy grasp' of the problem set? And, pointing the way to the next formal episode: how far can they pursue making draft plans, avoiding conflict and time-wasting?

The description of the above 'episode' essentially combines 'role-play' and 'out of role'. The fiction is to provide a mirror for self-reflection, a purpose to be seen by you *and* your class as critical. The 'episode' over, *as such*, the group will continue in their own time, with individual work in their journals, 'team' work drafting a plan. In a sense, it is only you, the leader, that has 'come out of role', for even in the fiction **they were themselves**, with their own names and identities. The fiction has merely endowed them with a context within which to carry out what is to be seen as an ongoing task – whether or not the leader is present 'being' a secretary to the Ambassador. They are now required to get a job done without the supporting presence of their leader. And it is their own job, under the umbrella of the metaphor which sheds light on their negotiation styles, choice of language especially in explaining something, expressing need or asking questions.

Communicating ideas to upper management

Let us look at the example where they are required to present their plans. A student (black, male) was brought in to play a 'full role' when this work was done with Northern Gas. You should try to bring in an 'outsider' for the role if possible. There are ways, less effective, round it if you cannot use anyone other than yourself or a cut-out figure.

E2. You ask your managers to wait [with their plans] outside the 'Ambassador's chambers' – and they are *in actuality* kept waiting outside their own room where the workshops are taking place. When you tell them [you are his secretary, of course] '*He is ready for you now*' What they see when they enter is a black, urbane ambassador, seated as a portrait in western dress, very sophisticated. His desk is meticulously arranged to indicate more than his own presence can reveal – photographs of family, papers referring to the enterprise, a glass and a carafe of water, a flag of Gongua on a stand etc.

On entry the managers use the convention of 'Stop time' [which the 'ambassador' is of course already using], a very useful convention when registration of detail is necessary. You ask each manager to say what he 'reads' of the scene and his expectations of the interview – and then you move it into 'now time' and improvisation starts, each spokesperson for the three teams presenting his plans. [You will watch carefully, as you hope the managers themselves are doing, for the *style* of the presentations – is there any hint of racism or patronising or lack of communication]? And when the meeting is over, there is much material for self and team analysis to resume.

When this work was done with Northern Gas, these particular managers were intrigued by the potential they saw in the exercise of 'reading' and so they wanted to look at their own working desks and the signals others might read and asked for more exercises related to this – a good example of how such emergent ideas can be incorporated if the session is not slavishly following a role-play plan. They began by selecting from a series of portraits and each portrait's 'desk' was then invented – others in the group went round the 'desks' guessing from what they 'read' how that person went about his/her work. They learnt about 'reading' as they hear each others responses and some had their eyes opened as to what they missed!

Here is an example of another related exercise:

'Find the person'
The managers were invited to 'read' two 'prepared' desks without knowing whose they were – except that they were 'real' people. One desk neatly displayed a catalogue of London Theatre Shows and

phone numbers written on a card attached, among other things a business person would be likely to need. The other contained a flask and some tapestry work in a transparent bag along with non-specific stationary and pens. They each gave their comments about the owner of the desk, some criticising the owners for having non-relevant items in what was a work space. The two owners of the desk appeared and took their places. The managers were invited to question them and it transpired that the theatre material was to hand because the personnel manager frequently had to arrange entertainment for European visitors to the firm. The person requiring embroidery used it to enable her to hold tutorials without pressurising students by looking earnestly into their eyes. [The managers labelled this exercise 'Find the person' and found it transferred to reading applications for positions and for interviewing in teams.]

Dealing with setbacks

Let's assume the teams have arrived in Gonga and have asked for an audience with a representative of the government, not knowing there has been a take-over. The test is how do your managers cope under unexpected circumstances? To do this episode you will need to have at least two actors available for a prepared scene.

E3... The teams have been working on detailed plans which they now assume they are about to present to the relevant government minister. Once more, you keep them standing outside, but this time they are to 'read' from sounds only, as though overhearing through an open door. What they hear are the ringing tones of two telephones being answered by a tense voice and the small sounds of metal on wood and of plates etc. You ask each in turn to 'read' what is going on.

Invited inside, they see a temporarily frozen picture: a soldier standing to attention; the country's flag laid on one side; an army officer with crumpled uniform and no tie, seated at desk in front of typewriter, a used plate with knife and fork; a can (opened) of rice and another of beans; a spike with dozens of messages poked on it. The officer, sitting on a straight-back chair, a large chair thrust on one side, was reaching for the telephone when the visitors came in and held the position while, the managers quietly in pairs shared what they are 'reading' and then reported their whispers to the whole group.

On a signal from you the still picture becomes a moving scene, so that the watchers can see the tensions expressed through actions such as the guard handing over more messages, hurriedly read and added to the spike. While the scene is being played each onlooker [and that is all they are, even when the still picture comes to life] writes down a personal note as to what they think their team should do about this new circumstance.

Leaving the 'scene' the managers confer on how they should respond. [**Note: they are not required to interact spontaneously with the actors in the scene** – the test is not about how well one or two spokespersons can think off the top of their heads in a novel social context, but how well they are able collectively to reassess their plans in the face of an expected situation.] They examine their individual written ideas and from these work out a cohesive plan.

Then the group interacts with the new régime, each team in turn negotiating with the tired officer according to their ideas, ideas which may vary from immediate requests to be flown back to the UK to the feasibility of carrying on with their plans on a smaller scale.

Following each interview, the three teams could then hear the officer comment to the guard on how *he* has been 'reading' *them*.

These are but a small selection of the episodes you would include on a sustained project of this kind. One of the dangers of such a long term episodic 'soap opera' is that you will become attached unhealthily to 'their play'. The saga is merely a support structure for a wide range of detailed, short exposures in which participants never lose sight of their main concern – in this instant, a team of colleagues developing team sense and team support.

F. Training hospital ward managers – using theatre.
Action in Management (AiM) include what they call 'Living Case Studies' in their programme of training through drama. The structure and focus of their presentation and the way they plan a typical training session, conducted by a facilitator, is worth examining in detail.

One of their programmes centres on the responsibilities of a hospital 'ward manager' (used to be 'ward sister'). Two actors have previously scripted and rehearsed an interaction between a ward manager and a nurse of lower rank who is called in to the office of the ward manager to be informally warned that her recent increase in short-term absences is near to the point of becoming a disciplinary matter.

There are three layers of meaning to the carefully prepared script and four levels of demand on the observers:

> **Meaning level One**
> **What is evident from the performance** – the audience of trainee managers observe a badly handled interview by a harassed ward manager and an over defensive nurse.

Trainee level One

1 A. After the performance the trainees, in pairs, note down good and bad aspects of the manager's behaviour

> **Meaning level Two**
> **What emerges from the 'hot-seating'** – the trainees as a whole group are invited to ask the 'characters' questions. They hear the facilitator explain to the characters that '...*there are some people here... who want to ask them some questions... who want to help...*' There is a layer of pre-prepared background information that the actors can gradually reveal under this kind of probing. In this case the audience learn that a past history of friendship has been soured by the unexpected promotion of one of them to manager six months earlier.

Trainee Level Two

2A. The trainees who have been uninihibitedly listing 'manager faults', now find themselves dealing with the manager as a person sitting there in front of them – with defences at the ready. Thus they are required to find out more without overtly criticising. They then interview a suspicious nurse whose instinct may be ready to clam up on these interrogators. Should the trainees' handling of the questions fail to bring out the 'hidden' information, the facilitator asks the 'right' questions for them, as the trainees will need the new information to go on to the next phase.]

Trainee level Three

Having heard the emerging information the trainees are formed into four groups of four – [16 is an ideal class size for this kind of study-group] – and are asked to prepare what advice they would give the 'ward manager'. **And the clock can be turned back**. The original interview can be replayed to accommodate the advice the trainees come up with. They have to work quickly, deciding in their small groups what is viable and distinguishing between mere cosmetic treatment and getting to the heart of the problem.

Meaning level Three
What emerges from the improved handling by the ward manager. The scene is replayed, the actor playing the manager trying to take the advice on board (even if she herself does not agree with it, she must do her best, for inappropriate advice must be exposed) and the other actor must keep her defensive role but be prepared to be disarmed should she judge the new approach by the manager is being effective. And this is where a third level of information may be revealed. Effective operation by the manager can expose a deeper aspect to the nurse's problem that neither the first run-through nor the 'questions' from strangers could possibly reveal.

Trainee level Four

The trainees' responsibility increases during this replay, for if any one feels that the agreed advice is not being followed a trainee can say STOP!; the action freezes; and the advice is re-explained. Likewise if they recognise their advice, once they see it carried out, has been inadequate, they can also stop the scene, admit to having been mistaken and try again. **Not only can time be interrupted but it can retreat to an earlier moment** in the scene, so that, unlike life, one can see one's mistakes, rub them out, and have life replayed in an amended form! Additionally, should the 'manager' be confused by unclear or conflicting directions she too can stop the scene and demand clarification. The focus of the replay is **primarily on the trainees** and only secondarily on the characters: how effective the manager is now depends directly on how effective the trainees are.

A follow up session can examine what the trainees have learnt. This could start in small groups, in which they evaluate themselves and each group could then report back to the whole class. If guidelines can be drawn up from the reporting back, the facilitator will be ready with flip-chart and pen.

The effectiveness of this approach to training lies in the stimulus of a well-prepared and convincingly performed drama. It qualifies as drama in that the scene has layers of hidden meaning which will remain unexposed let alone resolved unless one character behaves differently. What the audience sense is considerable unexplained tension which in a traditional play would gradually be accounted for as the play proceeds. In *this* work the 'hidden agenda' of one or more of the characters can only emerge when the *trainees* find the right key.

You might, as you read this, be wondering whether the participants on your courses could 'do this' themselves, dispensing with actors. This is unlikely as it would require very careful planning by you and rehearsing by them, for its real value lies in what is *not* said during the presentation. Even if they managed to create something convincing, it requires an unusual degree of perspicacity on the part of your actors to judge *when* and *how much* to adjust their behaviour to the changing style of management. The temptation for the actor is to 'spill the beans' too soon or to be so rapt up in being stubborn or defensive that s/he can't let go. If you wanted to try it without relying on a professional company such as **AiM**, very careful adaptation would be required and you could not hope to replace the professional actors.

References

1 Selzer, Richard *Confessions of a knife: Meditations on the Art of Surgery* London: Triad/Granada 1982 pp.18-19. (We wish to express our thanks to the author and publisher for permission to use these excerpts).

2. Action in Management, Castle Eden, County Durham TS27 4SX Phone/Fax (01429) 837257 e-mail: aim,drama@dial.pipex.com

CHAPTER THREE

DIMENSIONS OF ROLE-PLAY

If you have attempted to read through the examples of practice outlined in Chapters One and Two you probably feel over-faced and overfed with ideas and yet deprived of any sense of a basis for selecting from them. In this chapter we hope to help you arrive at such a basis. We will ask the question 'Are there detectable pathways along which one always goes in selecting a role-play for one's class?'

It would help to answer such a question if we could isolate *one* criterion for selection which could stand out above all others as indispensible to and absolutely integral to the nature of role-play when it is to be used in a learning context. If we could find that key criterion, any others would logically fall into place as sub-criteria supporting the central one. So is there one thing in common between doing safety drill in the school hall with infants and helping fresh medical students to consider aspects of the profession they have chosen? What does working with adolescents on an extract from Hamlet as a way of looking at 'disloyalty' have in common with an apprentice plumber practising showing his badge at a houseowner's front door?

All groups have to step into an 'as if' fiction, but it is a fiction conceived of by a tutor/teacher/leader or trainer in terms of *learning*. In other words what it is in respect of the two-fold fiction and learning outcome starts in *your* head – and *they* have to embrace it. Not unlike any other teacher/student modus operandum one would think, but requiring your students to role-play is uniquely challenging, for the 'embracing of knowledge' is not a matter of instruction or absorption: it is to be achieved by entering the fiction in a way that makes the required knowledge their own. When your class engage in role-play they are not *receiving* knowledge or *acquiring* knowledge but *making* it – and they realise that they are doing so. When they leave your session they do so recognising what they now know. This shift from the 'normal' passing on of knowledge to the 'making' of it **calls on ones humanness in a way not normally associated with an instructional context**. It is both challenging and exposing.

This, then, leads us to the key criterion for making a selection. The medium for learning is potentially an opportunity and a hazard. The single criterion on which you base your selection therefore is to get the balance right between taking that opportunity and protecting the learners. If you over-protect, they will not learn; if you under-protect they will not learn. Every decision you make will relate to striking the balance between **challenge** and **protection**.

If 'challenge/protection' represents our single criterion, let us now consider what the major logical sub-divisions might be.

Challenge/Protection

There appear to be those dimensions, (to do with how you see the subject to be learned, how you see your class, and what space and time you are going to work in) that affect your choice of role-play before you consider the nitty-gritty of what kind of role-play it should be. They are your 'givens', as it were, from which you have to work: – topic, class, space/time allocation.

Then there are those dimensions to do with what *kind* of role-play will be appropriate and what kind of preparation will be required.

And then what kinds of reflection will begin incipiently during the role-play, leading to reflective tasks consolidating the learning.

They divide simply into JUDGEMENTS YOU MAKE BEFORE THE ROLE-PLAY (from the 'givens'); CHOICE OF ROLE-PLAY; FOLLOW-UP. Thus you will need to consider how the right balance can be achieved between challenge and protection based on your perceptions before, during and after the role-play.

JUDGEMENTS YOU MAKE BEFORE THE ROLE-PLAY

A. **Dimensions relating to the topic itself, the class the space and time** [the 'givens'] – **ACCESSIBILITY, INVESTMENT AND FACILITIES**

Accessibility and Investment

What is the nature of what is to be learned? Is it an examination of a slice of behaviour, as in B5 (p. 18) in which malicious gossip is the subject? Or do you want your class to learn a job routine as in the first exercise we recommended for trainee gas-fitters who are required to repeat and learn a sequence of behaviours before getting out of a van. (D1 p.38)? Or is it to be an exercise in 'reading' others? Such experiences were central to the course for trainee doctors who had to 'read' their patients – see, for instance, the account by Richard Selzer used in Exercise C8a (pp.34-35). Or will the knowledge to be learned be put in the form of a problem to be solved, as in AiM's work with hospital managers (pp.53-56) where the participants on the course have to reconstruct the scene played between ward manager and nurse? Or is the best learning to be acquired through carrying out a task, as in A9 and 10 (pp.8-9) where the young children design an accident poster or duvet covers? Will the role-play tap knowledge they already have as in the early exercises for medical students in which they are required to make lists of, for example, what a doctor might carry around as part of his daily routine (C1a and b pp.24-25) or will they have to search for it, as in some of the Road Safety work where children will have to find out about the Highway Code and police procedures (A10-12 pp.9-11)? Is the purpose of the role-play to change habits, as in all the Road Drill exercise (A1 p.2) or to change attitude, as in the Northern Gas manager training where you want them to have a new respect for team interdependence? (pp.45-53) Is the knowledge to be gained to be filtered through a text, as in B2 Hamlet (p.15), B3 Othello (pp.16-18, and C8a Selzer (pp.34-35)?

Sometimes there is an intellectual problem. The written materials may make ambitious demands on the reading ability of your class. For instance, your Year 3 class may not be ready to cope with the reading skill required for the Road Safety Board Game (p.12). On the other hand it may be an emotional problem that makes it difficult for your class to make the condolence cards required for Exercise A6 (p.6) – it may be for some children too soon after losing a classmate. In either case you may feel there is not enough 'protection', leaving you with a choice of either abandoning those kind of exercises or taking 'several steps back' to ease your class into them. This 'taking several steps back' is one of the secrets of planning successful teaching. For instance in the Road Safety Game which requires pupils to place in order a sequence of events related to a policeman's duties obvious 'steps back' would be to begin with just, say, three items (perhaps written in simpler language) to be put in order. In the 'condolence' exercise you may structure the experience so that only those who are 'ready' need participate in the card-making.

Sometimes the topic is already a 'hot potato'. Those of you who have tackled racial abuse (see our attempt in Chapter 6) with a class for whom such abuse is a common experience will know how delicately one has to tread. We shall be looking at a similarly sensitive theme, the topic of 'bullying', later in this chapter. At the other extreme the topic may be *out* of the experience of the class. How do you introduce the text of Eliot's *Murder in the Cathedral* as an example of 'treachery' with a class of adolescents who have no conception of or interest in mediaeval religious values? Topics are open to trivialisation either because they seem too near the knuckle or too remote.

Or neither of these. It could simply be that the topic has no 'lure' for the particular group. When we first identified this particular dimension we just called it 'accessibility', but then realised that however appropriate the level of the topic it does not guarantee that your class will feel stirred by it sufficiently to want to participate. For instance, when Dorothy Heathcote worked with Volkswagon managers, one particular role-play involved a pregnant wife being driven to hospital by her husband – an event readily *accessible* to this group of married men with young children, but the *lure* was skilled driving of the truck! The appeal was that they had to simulate driving a vehicle while giving an advanced driver-commentary as they 'drove'. Thus the topic must be *both* accessible and attract your group's *investment*.

Looking at your class beforehand you will have some sense of their readiness to role-play and their 'social health'. You need to be aware of their 'point of view'. Many groups dread the thought of role-play, because they have previously had a bad experience or they think they are going to be required to 'act'. You are going to have to win their confidence. On the other hand you may be aware that there are people in your class who are natural 'destroyers' who will wreck any attempt at creative work. You are going to have to find a way of accommodating destructive behaviour or begin with agreeing a contract that 'we will let people get started'. Working in a prison, Gavin Bolton had three men in his group who quickly vocalised their antagonism to role-play ['Bloody rubbish!']. He managed to persuade them to keep quiet as he promised not to ask them to take part. Indeed they demonstrated their separateness by turning their chairs round and sitting with their backs to the circle the tutor and remaining group were sitting in. As the role-play proceeded however, they couldn't resist turning their heads to watch, and, because they knew they were not going to be called on to do anything, they, from the touchline, as it were, handed out advice as to 'what should happen next' in the fiction that was being created. There's a lesson about role-play in this anecdote!

This attitude of a class towards role-play is part of a bigger concept relating to the **cultural perceptions** already held by your class. Indeed it is such an important aspect of the use of role-play that a whole chapter (Chapter 5), called 'Who are you teaching?' will be devoted to it. Suffice here to explain that in addition to whatever fictional roles you want your class to try out, you will also have to consider (especially in terms of challenge/protection) what attitude they already bring into the classroom. For instance, they may view with suspicion any arrangement of chairs that looks like a 'lecture' or they may withdraw – psychologically, that is! – if they see they are to be required to read a text of any kind or, more deeply still, they may betray a cultural disposition that limits how they can perceive a particular role-play – for instance, their embedded view of promotion procedures at work may be sexist, racist or ageist.

All these aspects of your class's relationship with the chosen topic will be weighed up by you in terms of how far can you challenge them without making them vulnerable. You will of course discover that the more they trust you and the more they grow to trust the topic and themselves in role-play, the more you can take risks and make bigger demands of them.

Facilities and time

Space is another consideration before you can begin. It is of little use hoping to replicate a busy road of traffic with your Years 1 and 2 if you can't get use of the hall. It is of little use going into the hall if your class is going to be fazed by that amount of space. Heaven help you too if you can only work in a lecture hall with fixed seating or if you are offered the factory or school canteen for the hour before lunch! Another problem may be that you cannot prepare your space before-hand because someone else is using it. [And always respect others' use of the same space – leaving it ready for the next person]. Never, however, allow the allocated space to put you off. There is always a way of adapting your material. The authors of this book have experienced extraordinary locations, from narrow corridors to school-yards from huge gymnasia to a room in a house where the TV mustn't go off because Dad needed to watch the match! Add to this junk rooms, back of stage already set up for the school play, laboratories [with handy bunsen-burners] and domestic science rooms [with even handier oven knobs!].

Is the exercise to take but a few moments of interaction in order to supply a point of reference for discussion with your class, as in B8 (p.20) in which you in role address a member of your class about another girl's drug abuse? Or is it to be part of a sustained role-play sequence requiring a relatively large slice of time as in the project for Northern Gas Managers (pp.45-53)? Could it even be conceived of as a year's curriculum project in a primary school?

CHOICE OF ROLE-PLAY
B. Dimensions relating to role-play – Responsibility; Form; and Planning

Responsibility

Degree of responsibility comes most readily to mind, so that one finds oneself asking 'How much choice shall I give them?' Do you leave it as open as B6 (p.18) in which you simply instruct your groups to 'show an act of disloyalty', leaving form and content to them or do you specify in precise terms, as in the preceding exercise (B4 pp.17-18) where they are required to *sculpt* treachery, using characters from Shakespeare and, further, their voice overs, extracts from texts and images are to show the 'humanity' of the chosen characters?

You will also, within the traditional mode of role-play, think of degree of responsibility in respect of grouping – pairs? small groups? etc. Perhaps the major decision, however, relates to whether the work is to follow a traditional pattern or whether you want to start from the basis that your class are to be initiated into a *collective role* – in which case, are *you* going to *induct* them into their collective role by taking on a role yourself? A traditional approach is illustrated in A7 p.7, an exercise in which children in their pairs are invited to discuss and then 'show' to the others the reason why a child has suddenly run across a road, in spite of having learnt the Road Drill. Compare this with A4 pp.3-4 in which you address your class with '*Excuse me. I'm looking for K... S/he's always just here... Have you seen her...?*' Of course your decision about endowing your class with a *collective* role goes beyond a matter of *responsibility*: the whole question of how you want your class to engage with the relevant knowledge comes into play.

In the first two chapters we have attempted to cover the whole gamut of number arrangements from working on your own (D1 p.38) as in the 'gas-fitter' routine exercise to the leader addressing the whole class in role as 'secretary to the Ambassador of Gongua' (E1 p.49). Or there is the possibility of bringing in a 'full role' as in the same section (E2 and E4 pp.51-53). But there is also the matter of delegating 'directorial' responsibilities. In C8a and b (pp.34-35) work in pairs requires one medical trainee to 'direct' the other in how to replicate the patient in the anecdote. In D3. (p.43) the trainee gas-fitters are divided into three, one of whom is to 'direct' the other two, giving instruction cards to each. And when the scenes are shown to the rest, the audience are to assess whether the *director's instructions* were valid. In section F (pp.53-56). the hospital managers redirect the original scene.

How your class are to be expected to function is a fundamental aspect of 'responsibility'. We have mentioned under 'Accessibility and Investment', above, that your group may well betray a marked cultural disposition towards the topic or a prejudice against learning or role-play that will affect the baseline of any work you do. What you will also have to bear in mind is that the kind of role-play you choose and the very way you set it up will affect how your class will engage with the fiction, especially in respect of how much respon-sibility they are prepared to take on.

But what is to be their entry into the material? How *near* are they to be to whatever the event is – are they to be 'framed' as participants (I am *in* the event), commentators (I am telling you what is happen-ing), guides (I was there and I am recalling it for you), investigators, (I have the official authority to find out what happened) recorders (I am recording the event for all times), critics (I critique or interpret the event as an event) or as artists (I change the form of the event and remake it)? And having determined by selecting from this list of 'frames' the degree of distance and authority in relation to the event, what particular 'role' or 'entry into the material' do you want your players to have? Are they to be designers, historians, observers, en-quirers, explorers, storytellers, onlookers, inventors, reporters, wit-nesses, summarisers, editors, directors, commentators, writers of memoirs? If you choose the first 'frame', (participants actually *in the event*) which of the many kinds of status from employees to bosses, parents to offspring, police officers to members of the public, etc do you select? Choice of vocabulary, style of language, selection of material, body language and even whom they are allowed to address are factors controlled by the role they are to play. They have a responsibility to conduct themselves within the implicit rules of the chosen frame and the chosen point of view. In A4 (p.3-4) the young children are 'recalling' (no doubt vividly!) an accident to which they were onlookers. The freedom implicit in such an exercise contrasts markedly with A11 (p.10) in which, as curators of a Road Safety exhibition, they are required to describe the uses of their museum to a visiting teacher or with A12 where they are formal 'witnesses' at a hearing. They can influence only through the limits and opportunities each kind of 'entry' dictates. Thus when you are choosing a role for your class, among your first questions will be 'What kind and degree of responsibility do I want them to carry?' And you do this, fully aware that your choice will also affect the way they think and behave in the event and the quality of their learning.

So, it may not be enough just to select a role. You need to be aware of how you want them to be *framed*: that is, what *distance* from the actual event or what *authority* in connection with the event you want them to have. If you are setting them a task, your choice may be whether or not to endow them with a *role* in order to carry it out. Inviting your class to be, (as in B4 p.17-18) 'young sculptors' creating statues for a gallery of Shakespearean characters to represent 'treachery' is making very different demands on them and their classmates compared with asking them simply to direct [not in role] the scene between Iago and Othello (p.16-17) for the benefit of the rest of the class. In the former they may be required to justify their interpretation 'as sculptors'; whereas in the latter there is no such 'frame' controlling them. The chosen framing or the lack of it affects how they go about the task, how they explain what they are doing and how they are treated by others. The whole tenor of the exercise changes according to your choice.

In our chapter on 'Who are you teaching?' we will expand on the underlying *cultural* roles that reach beyond the particular 'framing'. The two concepts 'framing ' and 'cultural underpinning' together determine the quality of the experience.

Form

If we move to **Form** we come to perhaps the most exciting part of the decision-making, for here we have access to the whole range of theatre form, from the most obvious kind of improvisation as in B1d (p.14) where you want pairs to enact a scene related to a broken promise to the most elaborate form of script-making and showing, all within the fiction of it being part of a proposed TV programme on doctor/patient interaction – 'a play within a play' form of theatre (C9 p.35). Because it is theatre, attention must be given to 'signing'. (This will be discussed in detail in Chapter 4) Suffice here to draw attention to the wide divergence in precision of signing integral to the exercises in Chapters 1 and 2. Contrast the deliberate choice of casual signing required in D2 (p.40) in which the trainee gas-fitters, still sitting on their chairs, give token gestures to indicate actions with the elaborately prepared setting of the two offices (E2 and E4 pp.51 and 52-53 respectively) visited by the Northern Gas managers in Gongua.

But there are other dimensions of Form to be considered. They relate to 'time' and 'theatre *genre*'. There are at least six kinds of 'time' used in the preceding chapters:

TIME
The past recalled as narrative
In B1. (p.13) one partner is instructed to recall an incident from his/her past (relating to a betrayal of a secret). This is straightforward narration. Of course this particular example of role-play is about as uncluttered as one can get – as uncluttered as it is undemanding. But if the role were to be the imprisoned Guy Fawkes, thinking aloud as he writes his memoires about the betrayal by Lord Montargil of their arsonists' plan, or, alternatively, Guy Fawkes at a court hearing giving evidence or, Guy Fawkes dreaming of facing his Day of Judgement, recounting his sins, or a lecturer giving a historical resumé of the betrayal etc, each of these 'ways in' requires the narrative voice but the contrast in required style and selection of language and demeanour is marked.

Present actions mixed with asides in the past tense
In B7a (p.19) the two 'actors' use a mixture of past [to audience] and present in addressing each other:

Role of Pat: '...*our teacher called me aside..*

Role of teacher: '...*Pat could I have a word with you?...*'

The use of the present tense in a narrative accompanying virtual actions

In D2 (p.40) the trainee apprentices are to remain seated describing their 'actions' as if they are happening now:

'*I'm ringing the front door bell and I wait what seems ages... and the door is opened by this chap...*'

'Now' time

'Now' time is a common enough expression in drama referring either to the feeling by the participants in the fiction that 'it is happening now' or the impression built up by actors that what is happening on stage is happening now for the first time. It is not the 'now' of 'real' life, however, for events on stage are condensed into a compact present, even to the acceptance of such conventions as merely gesturing writing a letter or waiting at the end of a phone. B1d (p.14) in which two friends meet in an apartment typically requires the two players to interact as if it is happening now. This is especially reinforced by its being an improvisation, but however much the participants may feel 'it is happening now' there is an underlying artificiality of 'making a scene' which by definition distorts time. This is why you should not assume that all your classes are ready to work in 'now time', for that artificiality requires a degree of technique, a point that is often overlooked by drama enthusiasts who do not realise that others feel vulnerable when asked to participate. There may be occasions, of course, when it is appropriate to invite groups in your class to rehearse and 'perform' with all that implies of entertaining the others [see our comments following A8 (pp.7-8) relating to the young children's stylised 'performance' of the road accident.]

However, when the tutor/teacher takes a role s/he can carry the burden of that technique and allow the class to feel that it is indeed 'happening now'. If we look at A4 (pp.3-4) in which the teacher plays the role of an anxious parent looking for a child. When she says *'Excuse me, I'm looking for K...'*, the class respond in the 'natural' here and now of answering someone's questions.

'Now time' with implied 'demonstration'

Another use of 'now time' that reduces embarrassment and vulnerability is for the tutor to insist, as in many of the examples we have listed, that the improvisation should be seen as a *demonstration* – of a procedure, of an interpretation, of an argument, of a typical example of something, of a memory, of an incident, of a hypothesis etc. In other words, although it occurs in the present tense, there is an edge to the whole presentation that is signalling to a group of scrutineers: 'Supposing, it were *thus...*' And the 'thus' takes it out of the present tense into a kind of *subjunctive* tense. C7 (pp.30-31) is a good example. The players in pairs are given out printed instructions about the doctor/patient role they are to play in which the doctor is to give the patient news that the illness or injury is more serious than first thought. They are invited to try this out a number of times, feeling their way into quality communication between them. They are playing it in the 'here and now', but the scene is continually being held up for inspection, even as it is happening and the mode is one of 'supposing *it were thus...* what *would be* the strengths and weaknesses of such an interaction?'

'Real' time

This is the time that belongs to task-centred work, for actual tasks have to be completed as part of the problem solving or the 'enterprise' fiction. Thus, the 'expert poster-makers' will in actuality make posters for display (A9 pp.8-9) and the Northern Gas managers (belonging to a problem-solving genre other than 'Mantle of the Expert, but carrying similar responsibilities) will carefully prepare their plans for Gongua and *in actuality* amend them when political circumstances change.

THEATRE *GENRES*

You have to find the theatre form that will find the right balance between getting most out of the material and exposing the vulnerable side of your class. Again over-protection can lead to under-achievement. Sometimes the topic itself can appear just undemanding. This may well be because the *form* you have chosen fails to do justice to the material. For instance, merely to enact the kiss of betrayal in the Garden of Gethsemane (B9 p.20) without slowing down the pace for carefully controlled movement and commentary invites limited effort from the players as they turn a hugely significant event into a naturalistic representation of an action that is over in seconds.

The use of 'Depiction' [see A8 pp.7-8 in which the six K's sign a different phase of a road accident with teacher speaking the thoughts associated with each one], 'Freezing or interrupting the flow of a scene' [in section F. p.55, the trainee hospital ward managers can stop the replay of the scene at any time in order to give further advice to the players; in E2. (p.51) the Northern Gas managers can use 'Stop time!' in order to register detail] and 'Chamber theatre' [See the chapter 4 on 'Signing'] are all theatre forms suitable for slowing down the action for the sake of making significant meaning and drawing attention to detail. It is interesting that the required attention to detail and precision is itself protective. It frees your participants from the 'artistry' of 'improvising' a credible scene 'out of nothing', as it were.

Another way of requiring your class to stop and think is, of course, the use of a dramatic script, so that *interpretation* becomes an initial step as in the work on *Hamlet* and *Othello* [pp.15-17]. If you feel your class can cope with this way in, you will also appreciate that it gets over the problem of your retaining the power. The *text* now dictates. Very popular among traditional role-play and simulation leaders is the use of an *instructional* 'script'. We have included an example in C7. (p.30) where 'doctor' and 'patient' receive their printed text. In task-centred work there are other kinds of written texts and imagery that can act as stimuli to belief in the work. Further than that, such a text signals emphasis on *detail* and continues to be a point of reference. In order to begin the Gongua metaphor with the Northern Gas managers, their way in to the problem is through an 'authentic' letter and a map of the fictional country.

The very nature and style of the objects they use must have what can be called 'internal coherence'. We have a good example in the introduction of the 'map' of Gongua (p.48). It has to stand up as 'believable' in respect of quality of materials and workmanship and in respect of amount of careful detail, and yet it had also to signal that it is part of a fiction. As we said in the second chapter, a genuine map with a name change would not have satisfied a proper sense of internal coherence. We shall come across many examples of appropriateness in choice of 'signs' in Chapter 4.

Planning

All the previous considerations of topic, class, responsibility and form will now place you in a position of planning your class' engagement with the material. You will have to decide whether and to what extent it will be necessary to conduct non-drama experiences before starting role-play. These may take the form of discussions, games, studying documents, maps or diagrams, examining an artefact or watching a performance.

FOLLOW-UP
C. Reflection

This is absolutely critical to the work. It is the final chance for the participants to recognise and reassess what has been learned, to know and to know what they know. We say 'final' chance, for as will have been appreciated in the examples so far, self-spectatorship of this kind is built in to the structure of the role.

So, having made a list of so-called 'dimensions', how do we suggest you use them? The answer is that it depends on your purpose. If you want to give a general guidance to others on the use of role-play with a particular topic, then we could see you combing through the 'Dimensions', picking out all the relevant aspects, so that your advice is as complete as possible. If, however, you are a practitioner, faced with doing this role-play with a class tomorrow, then you will no doubt follow your intuition and immediately gather images of possible action. What we suggest in this latter case is that, *if* you have time to ponder and refine, you could, with your intuitive plan sketched out before you, now pick up the 'Dimensions' and check some of the logic of what you have planned. This may confirm what you have done or jolt you into recognising a flaw or even add something to your scheme. We could call these two approaches the 'intellectual way' and the 'intuitive way', or simply 'head' and 'heart'.

Let's see how this works out with a lengthy example. We'll take the theme of 'Health Education', select one aspect of it and use the 'head' approach and then a number of different aspects using the 'heart'!

Health Education

Let's take a component of a compulsory part of the *National Curriculum*, **Health Education**, an umbrella subject covering mental and social aspects, as well as physical:

The supporting government documents on the subject offer the following objectives:

> The National Curriculum for Health Education offers opportunities:
>
> to acquire knowledge
> to explore their own knowledge
> to explore their own and others' attitudes and values [mentions role-play here]
> to learn skills to make informed choices
> to establish a healthy life-style
> to build a system of values.

It is perhaps significant that the writers of the above list of objectives see a place for the use of role-play in relation to 'attitudes' and 'values'. Fine, we agree. But what about **knowledge**? As you will have realised in reading this book so far, we are concerned with the use of role in the acquisition of information *and* in grasping the underlying values of such information. However, there is also a place for using it to examine social attitudes and values, so we will begin with a stark example of social ill-health – bullying.

Bullying – using the 'Dimensions' list to get a general picture of how one might approach this difficult subject. [The 'head' approach]. We remind ourselves that the dimensions were **Accessibility of topic; Investment of class, Facilities; Responsibility; Form; and Planning Reflection**

We need to consider each in turn basing our decisions on the **challenge/protection** criterion.

This is one of those dangerous topics the dramatic representation of which may actually *perpetuate* the behaviour you are trying to be rid of. You may feel fully justified in choosing such a topic but your class may have its own sinister agenda. Thus you need to be aware from the beginning of your planning that naturalistic representation, in which current classroom power structure could unwittingly be replayed, is to be avoided and that *your* agenda will be clearly preset through the presentation of *written* materials [such as case-studies; reports or letters] with the students *framed* as some kind of professionals required to carry out a series of tasks. Whatever the hidden power relationships within the class, their attention will be drawn from the start to issues arising from the fictitious people referred to in the provided documents and your students' roles will not be that of the bullies or the bullied – unless they, *as professionals*, require to illustrate bullying incidents for themselves, in which case such non-naturalistic devices as cut-outs; commentary; slow motion; actor narration etc will be available.

Thus your thinking, logically and necessarily, starts to follow the **dimensions**:

Relating to the topic itself (Accessibility): close to the emotional surface for your class; open to abuse. Your purpose will inevitably relate to changing the attitude of your class.

Relating to the participants (Investment): your particular group of students may have their own history of bullying either as inflictors or victims – or both.

Where major responsibility is to lie (Responsibility): teacher/whole class with the early steps of the programme. You may be in role as a 'fellow professional' or as a 'worried headteacher', but as leader of the role-play, you will continually monitor your students' level of engagement with the material. Should it involve setting tasks in pairs or small groups, you will be 'omnipresent', as if requiring their 'findings' or seeking their 'advice', but in effect taking full responsibility for the respectful way the tasks are carried out. Teacher responsibility with this kind of topic is paramount. What you are *not* going to do is to lay the responsibility on members of your class to improvise a bullying incident. Your class' engagement with role will be a *collective* responsibility.

Relating to form (Form): go for the non-naturalistic. Use those kind of dramatic forms [depictions or rituals or Mantle of the Expert] when *time* can be slowed down or stand still. It is the *commentaries* that create the thoughtful work, the 'voice-over' or the written label or the alter ego or the freezing of action. If you choose the 'Mantle of the Expert' approach, the focus of attention is securely on some 'client's' needs and if some kind of representation of bullying is needed, it will be in their roles as *professionals* that carry out the dramatic illustrations – a role within a role. This double role not only provides a safety measure for carrying out the project, but its *prismatic* mirroring of bullying events carries a greater potential for enhanced insight into the complexity of the topic. With a sensitive topic like bullying one is immediately aware of possible abuse if naturalistic representation is encouraged, but such a form of representation carries a more fundamental weakness: unless the representation is created by relatively experienced actors its meaning rarely goes beyond 'what happened', a uni-dimensional level that cannot in itself challenge the thinking of participants or audience.

The devising and planning (Planning): you will need to decide beforehand whether from the outset you want the class to *know* that they are investigating bullying or whether they are to arrive at the conclusion that it is an incident of bullying that is emerging from the documents they are studying. Whichever of these seems appropriate, you will recognise that a low key start is required. You may begin by inviting them to do something as ordinary as underlining the key words of a text, say, a newspaper editorial on the scale of increase in bullying or a report on the psychology of the bully or a parent's letter to the school governors or inviting them to list new school rules for bullying avoidance or a letter or a report that appears to be an account of, say, 'truancy', leaving the class gradually to spot that what it is *really* about is 'bullying'.

Reflection, review (Reflection): absolutely critical with this kind of issue. It does not have to take the form of a discussion. It could be 'a report of findings', written individually or in groups. All the better if there is some legitimate audience to whom the report can be sent. Of course, it is possible that the final reflection could take a dramatic form in which small groups present their conclusions visually/orally. In this case, the *final* review lies in the class' and teacher's opportunity for comments, drawing attention to significant perspectives.

Thus, one might go through the 'head' process, arriving at guide-lines on how to conduct sessions in schools on 'bullying'. Before looking at the 'heart' approach, let us add one or two points relating to the conditions under which 'bullying' might become the theme for a conference.

The above represent the kinds of thinking you are likely to find yourself adopting if, say, your school was launching a blitz on bullying. But there may be circumstances especially set up to deal with the problem – say a conference for teachers or, as recorded in *Countering Bullying* by Seamus Farrell and John Lampen[1], a 'Peace Project' to which Primary Schools in Londonderry were invited to send two *pupils*. The day's project was to be on the subject of 'bullying' and the second half was devoted to the use of role-play in which groups were simply invited to make some scenes representing typical school bullying episodes in preparation for showing them to the rest of the conference for discussion. The scenes were stopped at key moments: 'At the crisis point they paused and asked the audience for its comments and ideas and then presented their solution in dramatic form.' (p.154)

Now this appears to have been a typical use of role-play, in which participants 'think up a scene'; 'prepare it for showing'; 'show it'; 'invite discussion' at some point. Here the young participants are being invited to employ the very form of naturalistic behaviour that we, in the above paragraphs, have been avoiding on the grounds of possible abuse and/or of superficiality of meaning. Indeed one can imagine some of the banal dramatisation that actually went on. And yet, from the published report of the conference it clearly produced intelligent discussion and creative ideas for how a school might tackle the problem in the future. So here we appear to have a paradox.

It is what we referred to under the dimension of 'Investment' above as 'point of views', that has become the key to this paradox. The group have already been brought together specifically for the issue. Thus the *context* is purposefully defined by the subject-matter and the cultural identity of the people attending to it. The participants already bring 'a point of view', *authorised* by the event. They bring to their witnessing of the role-play a readiness to explore and a knowledge to be tapped. The outcome is that the surface meaning provided by the naturalistic presentation serves as a catalyst for triggering other more searching levels of meaning. The nine-year old children, tacitly framed as they are in this one-day conference as people sharing a knowledge of bullying, are ready to see beyond the immediacy of an incident played out and to look at the implications or consequences of such an incident. It is not the case, as perhaps readers assume, that presenting the dramas or witnessing the dramas are *in themselves* significant. They are merely devices for opening up a topic with a group who already, by virtue of their tacit role in attending the conference, are in a particularly receptive and creative frame of mind.

And this is an opportunity to mention role as **therapy**. There is not space within this book to cover therapy, but the chance to define it logically follows from the above example in which it is 'understood' that the participants have a deep *knowledge* to bring to the subject, an *intellectual disposition*, as it were, alongside their emotional agendas. Therapy is also dependent on a tacit framing of the participants, but in therapy it is *understood* that the partipant(s) brings a personal hurt, perhaps already very near to the surface, perhaps deeply disguised, alongside an intellectual grasp of the subject. And the most superficial role-playing can serve sometimes as a catalyst; this time however not for further intellectual probing, but for the expression of that hurt. Both groups are framed by their identification with the subject-matter.

Other aspects of Health Education: thinking up lesson plan drafts *and then* checking with the list of 'Dimensions' – the 'heart' approach.

Topic – 'School Dinners' [Grades 1/2]

> This involves a classroom table covered with white drawing paper on which you draw the outline of big serving dishes, blank labels for each child and labels for the dishes. Your class draw or stick pictures of their choices of food into the dish outlines while you give each dish a name: e.g. potatoes – baked; fish – fried; fish – baked; etc. You fill in their blank labels with the right words as each child decides on the kind of food s/he likes for school lunch. In role as the 'dinner lady' you invite them to 'queue up' for their food [you've given them paper plates] which you serve from the appropriate dish – with real serving spoons. Back in their seats they draw their choice of food onto their plates. All are displayed. You and children together then make a graph or bar chart of 'food choice'.

Using the 'Dimension' monitor of accessibility, investment, facilities, responsibility, form, planning and reflection, of particular interest is the social health of the class (Investment) which may not easily cope with either the 'queueing' or the keeping to a choice. Indeed you may have chosen this particular format in anticipation that it will offer practice in orderliness for some of them. It is a good exercise for beginning the diet aspect of Health Education as its purpose is to raise consciousness of the familiar (Accessibility). Food is to be thought of *as* food – and then it is brought under a different lens when the class 'graph' is made. Here is an example of simple, undemanding, brief teacher-led role-play (Form), repeating a routine activity in 'now time', that will continue to **feed** [excuse the unintended pun!] all kinds of knowledge – and they see their teacher 'being both teacher and dinner lady' (Responsibility and Form), a composite role they are going to have to get used to! Their own identity is a *collective* one – they are to be 'a class of children'.

Notice where the role-play comes in the sequence of the plan – it is, typically, a 'role-play' *sandwich*, layered between word labelling and representations [the drawing and the graph]. This mixture of the scripted [written words], expressive [role] and iconic [picture] is a combination that will appear regularly in our role-play. The graph work obviously demands a totally different frame of mind on the same subject. It is a good example of using the knowledge emerging from the role-play experience and transforming it into a different medium. This is a key to the modern application of learning through role – it is how you refilter it that marks the true educator. As they do their graphs, the kinds of understanding emerging from the recent role-play are not suddenly dropped, but become reabsorbed and re-understood – and extended.

Now an example on food for older pupils:

Topic – 'Digesting – keeping the body machine running well' [Key Stage 2]

You will need to set up an outline of a human form on a table, a child's body, correctly proportioned. Your class are going to put into place the various digestive organs from mouth/teeth/tongue to bladder. They will do this having researched [in groups, from quality resources] their particular organ's name and function.

You will need to establish two contexts, the educational one, that this is the launching of a long-term Health Education Programme and a fictitious Mantle of the Expert context, set in a 'Medical School' that allows them to carry out the task as part of 'preparing a lecture' for others to learn from.

Each group will prepare its lecture – which will be carried out with an invited audience such as a few parents, another teacher or other children. The audience will be able to ask questions.

This kind of role-play deals with 'things as they are', transforming unfamiliar factual knowledge (Accessibility) into owned ex-perience. You hope the seeming seriousness and status of the 'Mantle of the Expert' approach will win their interest (Investment) and overcome their natural inclination to treat the subject in a jokey, trivialising manner. You will have to decide whether you want pupils to *design* the model, cutting out shapes of organs themselves or whether it is better to have these already at hand. Notice that the role-play operates entirely in **real time** (Form). [Compare this with the 'now time' of the infant exercise when they were queueing up for school dinner – with a *token* serving demonstrated by their teacher.] They will in actuality, in their collective role of 'medical assistants', be carrying out the tasks and use may be made of the 'real time' pressure of '*Just look at the time... I hadn't realised we were running late... our audience will be here soon*' to increase a sense of responsibility for each 'team'. Quality of learning (Accessibility) may partly depend on the usefulness of the audience's questions. It may be possible to prepare the audience beforehand.

Topic: The concepts of 'happiness' and 'health' – Key-Stage One

You discuss with your class what being 'happy' and then what being 'healthy' means. Draw a large round face with a smile in the middle of your blackboard or flip chart, writing a heading, 'happy' and 'healthy' each side of drawing. With the aid of your class you make a list of 'happy' and 'healthy' suggestions.

You then take up a 'baby' and explain this is a new prince/princess [there could be twins!] and the King and Queen have asked all the people to come and make good wishes so the baby can grow up happy and healthy.

Each pair is allowed one wish only, one from each column. You then organise a ritualistic coming up to the baby [the 'happy' wishes first and then the whole ritual will be repeated for the 'healthy' wishes], each pair explaining to all the other well-wishers their choice of wish and the reasons for their choice, with you, holding the 'baby', and with your gentle questions prodding, if necessary, for fuller explanations – and a total National Curriculum in Health Education is opened!

Now here is an example of using role that can only grow out of the children's background experience where you have already shared a Fairy story-telling about Princesses and Wishes! (Accessibility), so that what you are now doing seems to your pupils to arise naturally out of 'that story we read the other day'. But in the above, before you create the 'baby', you have made *personal* connections (Investment) with individuals who will have their own experiences to be tapped.

You may find the two terms 'happiness' and 'health' are just not separable in some pupils minds [when the tooth-ache goes I feel happy!], but this does not matter; the purpose of the exercise is to put forward the idea that such abstract concepts can be related but different. It is a beginning of conceptual analysis reinforced through the enjoyable experience of a ritual (Form).

There is another form of teaching built into this exercise which you may care to expand should you think it appropriate. You could place the emphasis on word recognition with a class in which there are non-readers. Indeed the 'wish' game could be part of the 'literacy hour'.

The pupils have choice (Responsibility) and that choice is made public (Form). They are both seen and see in turn. Notice too how the ritual allows moments to be 'held' for reflection. This is where your choice of role for yourself allows you to operate as a teacher within it (Responsibility), seizing the chance within the moment of the action to both honour what is being offered and draw attention to its significance.

Now let's take up a similar theme 'making wishes for someone's future' for much older children, say, Grades 7/8.

Topic: 'Good Parenting' [Key Stage Two]

You and your class have been collecting pictures (modern) of children as if they are in need of adoption. Together you invent their histories and put them in files. Then, taking on the role of 'Social workers' or 'Adoption Society people' you consider selected case-files and from the stories they have invented and prepare a handbook (or better still, a video) to help adopting parents deal with parenthood.

For example, you may all regard a picture of a crying child and from this make a list of the many reasons why children cry – pain, loneliness, wanting to be picked up, frightened, hungry, wet etc and then demonstrate these examples to a small audience of adults – instructing them on how to deal wisely with each of these.

Alternatively, the selected picture could be of a child near a cooker, bath, unlabelled bottles, pan handles etc – and your class demonstrate potential dangers.

> Or, closer to 'adoption' theme, photographs of ethnic children – what will the new parents need to understand about the country the child has come from? – climate, customs, songs, foods, stories , history, legends. (This might be an entry into the theme of racial prejudice which we will be dealing with in Chapter 6)

Your class (collectively) may find it easier directly to *teach* rather than *demonstrate* to a small audience, so on the topic of how parents keep children safe you might take on the role of a 'robot' whose job was to make a house safe for children when a parent was out at work. The children have to train the robot to clear dangerous things out of reach, lock cupboards, avoid hazards outside.

And focusing on 'healthy living' rather than 'safety' a good parenting exercise might look like this:

> You have collected a whole range of pictures of children of all ages and nationalities doing things related to healthy living – sports activities; hygiene routines; eating and drinking; sleeping; hobbies; studying; being with friends; laughing with family; 'working out' in the gym, and being in the open air etc. Tell your class, as they look at a panorama you have made of the pictures, that in a while you will be putting them in role as people who have an expertise relating to these pictures. Can they guess what that expertise will be? *'Children? Yes... something more... etc'* and you may or may not have to tell them that the collection represents 'healthy living'.
>
> Now invite the class, not in role yet, to classify the pictures under 'healthy living' headings. Then pose the question as to whether each of these activities shown could in fact become the *opposite* of healthy living. Can they think up scenarios when each of the same activities actually *undermines* health?
>
> Now explain their collective role of Social Workers who interview people who want to adopt a child. They are to interview two potential applicants – and you hand over the curriculum vitae of two young women. This interview, one of a series, is to check the candidates' knowledge of 'healthy living'. You give 'the expert panel' time to prepare the areas of questions they think ought to be asked, relating to the pictures they have already been discussing. You will now play

the role of each of these women in turn, making them equally personally attractive, but each will have a blind spot [a different blind spot] connected with some area of health.

The task for the 'interviewers' is which one to choose. The 'real' task is to recognise inadequate understanding of some health issue. After the interviews, you can let them have 'free for all' discussion or you could 'come in' as a senior colleague who wants to know what criteria they will now apply in choosing between two otherwise equally qualified applicants. They may choose neither!

The object of this exercise is to widen the concept of 'healthy living' and to create an awareness of the dangers of excess in normally positive activities. There are two 'fun' aspects to this (Accessibility), not in the topic itself, but in the structure you are giving it – having to guess what their role might be; and enjoying you playing two roles which can only be distinguished in terms of health priorities. You will appreciate that the process of making a choice (Reflection) can be pitched at either a casual or tightly structured level according to what you feel your class are ready for.

Extending the idea of 'child carers':

Start as an agency set up to validate those who want to work with children. An early task would be to list types of carers – nannies, nursery school helpers, crêches, baby-sitters etc. It is the agency's job to interview applicants.

Supply a range of pictures of children engaged in different kinds of activities, from sports to eating and label the potentially good and less good aspects of each picture.

And then consider how each of these activities should be supervised by a competent carer.

Prepare possible questions for interviews, perhaps relating them to the very pictures you and 'your colleagues' have already examined – to see whether the interviewee 'reads' the picture fully. And you could also show the interviewee a letter from a parent outlining a problem e.g. 'my daughter doesn't like ...'

Topic: Safe Children Compounds – War Zones [Key-Stage 2/3]

> You have an air-ticket to take you out, as part of a volunteer service, to Albanian or Macedonian camps for children who have lost or been separated from their parents as they crossed the border from Kosovo. Your concern is to ask advice from your class about how one can best help children (younger than your class!) to survive in these extreme circumstances. How to keep them occupied? What stories, what songs? what games? tools? toys?... Your class select which to consider and break them down into a classification. For instance games may be considered as a way of making friends, a way of passing the time, a way of sharing, taking turns, getting back concentration, regaining self-esteem. You ask them to make posters for you to put up in camps as advice.

They can then give you advice about the best ways of telling or reading a story to a group – how to collect the children together, the kind of voice to use, how to talk about it afterwards, is there a best time of day? how to get them to make up stories.

Topic: Robinson Crusoe photo archive [Grades 3/4].

> Assuming this is a continuing part of your Health Education project, you might introduce this theme by saying 'It's all very well us talking about keeping healthy, but how does **this** chap manage?' – and you show a picture of a man whose story they already know – Robinson Crusoe. You invite the class to join you in making a model of his island. As they build it, you open up a discussion of all those aspects they have covered in Health Education, but now you are saying: 'So how did he clean his teeth, wash, shave, dispose of uneaten food to keep his camp free of flies, protect himself from the sun and torrential storms, deal with cuts, deal with loneliness and know what things can be eaten safely?'
>
> You now invite your class, in small groups, to demonstrate [still pictures] some of their answers to these questions. You use a polaroid type camera to snap these so that they can be put in a book or on a chart [advice to sailors who might get shipwrecked or to a solo adventurer sailing round the world?] with written instructions underneath each photograph. The photos can be classified under shelter, escape plans, hygiene, safe eating etc.

The Robinson Crusoe context will have instant appeal (Accessibility). It is a good example of recreating known knowledge by placing it in an unfamiliar context. This time the 're-creation' will promote 'back to basics' solutions, paring away all elaborate manufactured resources. Having to present a 'still picture' of an action (Form) for a photograph focuses their minds on particular, precise questions. The quality of talk you engage in as you assemble the model will provide the foundation for serious thinking about the problem. Notice again that we have a 'role-play sandwich' – this time, model-making, followed by creating still pictures, followed by writing instructions [or instructing *you* what to write] under the photographs.

Topic: Remember you were once a child [young adolescents]

Mental, physical and social health looks differently from different age perspectives. When the old have to understand the young in terms of these needs and the old the young, it takes a conceptual shift that many are not ready for. It may be that changing the perspective is a way of illuminating the National Curriculum's Health Education. There is a wide and varied potential in such a long-term project. Let us give an example of an old person seeking that aspect of mental health we call 'peace of mind'.

If you intend it as a long-term project you will create with your class a map of a housing estate, for which you can gradually invent characters of different ages and places such as local shop, school, small businesses. We will start with some children and an elderly widow living on her own, her house by an alley-way and her front garden onto the cul de sac end of the street the children mostly live in or near.

You show your class a series of letters of complaint from this old lady to the Council about small children noisily and destructively playing, even after dark, just outside her house and down the alley-way. The council want to use your class to demonstrate to the old lady [it is going to be you in role!] what 'playing' *means* in terms of growing up.

You ask your class what do they think 'small' ['little kids' to your adolescents of course!] children would typically play. You then proceed to guide them into analysing the selected game, just as a game, not yet in the context of playing in the old lady's neighbourhood. You list its social ingredients. If they have chosen 'football', [it could be skipping while singing loudly or riding bikes at speed] it might include items such as 'keeping to the rules', 'deciding the limits of the pitch'; 'positioning the goal post', 'choosing a goalie', 'not keeping the ball to yourself', 'competing', 'whose ball is it?' and 'making sure it is returned home when play finishes', 'searching for ball if it gets lost', 'arguing and agreeing about decisions', 'no fighting' etc.

Now, you ask them to consider, before 'meeting' the old lady all those aspects where the requirements of the game conflict with the peace of mind the old lady is seeking. They should also try to anticipate what the old person's reactions will be. You then 'become the old lady' who has agreed to listen to what a group of children have to say.

The fiction of the old lady's letters provides a stimulus [Investment] for consideration of quite a complex range of concepts – the nature of the game itself, especially those qualities relating to social health; the old lady's perspective on the game and *her* need for mental [*and* social!] health; and how can useful communication occur? The Form of the role-play makes little demand on your class but the Content is challenging for them. The effectiveness of the handling of the content will depend to some extent on the sensitivity and subtlety of *your* role. Within the narrow scope of 'an old lady with a complaint' you must find a way *in your teacher function* to open doors for your class while appearing to close them. So you will have to *inadvertently* give your class an opening. For instance, '*...they don't know how to bring children up these days...*' is suitably negative within the old lady's frame of mind, but might well become a positive introduction to the topic of the social health needs of young children.

Topic: Making things Grow – the food cycle (many ages)

Some items under the heading of the National Curriculum's Health Education may have little appeal (Accessibility). This could be one such – especially with city children (Investment) who may have no interest in or direct experience of the Seasons and their affect on growth. So, how do you stimulate your class sufficiently for them to carry out research on material that may be unfamiliar – and 'boring'!?

One possibility is to challenge them to create a collage of images and sound, using movement, dance, and spoken words to convey a seasonal cycle. The Purpose would have to satisfy more than the Health Education syllabus; it would have to meet what your class were already working at in their Physical Education curriculum.

Another possibility is to continue with the 'letter to the Council' stimulus used in 'Remember you were once a child'. This time a letter about a neglected allotment could be taken up by your class in a Mantle of the Expert role as 'Garden Advisers' to a newly retired or redundant person.

Topic – 'Being a Compost Heap' [Key Stage 1]

From pictures of all kinds of food your pupils select which left-overs they think they should become in order to have the privilege of being thrown [in 'movement' by you, the 'gardener'] onto the compost heap. A series of large movements of sun, rain, turning of heap, worms eating, and bacteria growing in heat transforms the heap so that it can be spread on the garden. As they learn about the scientific changes they can make up songs or commentaries about nature's work. The whole work becomes a 'nature ballet' or 'dance story' or even a 'folk opera'.

Topic – 'A house is not a home until...' [Grade 2]

You're going to begin with the notion of a 'house' that has to have things in it, to a 'home' that has to have things happening in it.

You will probably need to introduce the idea of a 'plan', so that you may start with drawing the outline of your classroom and its relationship to another shape – the corridor, and its relationship to another one – the school hall. Then you move to showing where things are in our classroom. From this, you can move to your main purpose, drawing a plan of a room in a house, but you are not going to do this straightforwardly. You are going to be 'a dreaming architect' who draws in his sleep; he draws the room that children whisper to him. [you'll prearrange that your class select a room without you knowing what it is to be and you'll also pre-plan the order in which children can creep up and whisper to you what is to go into the room.] When you've finished the drawing you give it a big title: *A kitchen* [or whatever] *in a house.*

Your dream over, you leave the drawing for 'the teacher' to see. The architect 'goes out' and 'teacher' returns. You show interest in the 'room in the house' and go over what has been put in it. Now you take up another big sheet of paper, the same size and you write at the top *A kitchen* [or whatever] *in a **home,** musing 'I wonder if that architect will know what goes into a home or does he just know about things going into a house?... Perhaps you could show him...What would you show him, if we asked him to come back and have another dream?... what makes a home?*

You now get the class to think up some of the things families do at home. Small groups will select one example and then 'teacher' fetches the 'architect' who dreams and asks questions as he dreams about why these things make it a 'home' and, of course, you know you are eventually going to pose the question: '*I wonder what people do in their houses to make sure they grow up healthy?*'

We have placed the emphasis on 'a room' in a house rather than a house as your pupils may come from widely contrasted housing (Investment). If you know they all come from the same housing estate then the whole plan can be drawn which makes a better basis for considering 'home'. Nevertheless there is a danger with a topic of this kind of promoting teacher's middle class image and even if you manage to steer aspects of what goes on in a home towards healthy living, you may get answers you do not expect.

Another aspect affecting degree of Investment is the social health of the class. If yours is the kind of class that will take advantage of your vulnerability when you become the 'dreaming architect', – for you have temporarily lost your normal 'Johnny, don't do that!' power. Such a class may need first to make their own room drawings which they hand to 'the secretary' who will leave them, on your class's behalf, in the 'architect's office'. A chair back labelled '*Architect – out to lunch*' would then permit you to 'phone your boss' saying the plans had been left. *Then* you may get a contract with your class that you are going to become the 'architect' now and 'he' will examine and comment on their plans. 'The architect', with a carefully modulated voice, will raise more questions [about *house* only at this stage] than they will have thought of. For instance, '*Two windows in the kitchen – I wonder if it's best to have them both overlooking the garden or whether I should put them in separate walls with a different view for each?*'

Whichever approach you use, you are going to require small groups to prepare to show the architect what goes on in a home. For this kind of demonstration which entails indicating a *place*, your class will discover the need to *sign* [in the 'theatre' sense of 'sign' (Form)], ranging from the simple signs such as '*what shall we use as a bed?*' to the more complex '*If this person is feeling upset I wonder how we can show that, even if she isn't in the house just yet?*' Problems like this can be very daunting if a teacher thinks you have to have realistic objects. But if you look for an appropriate choice of 'sign', even, for example an image as strong as a trashed room left by the upset person, can be created with a TV set with crack in its screen, drawn on sugar paper taped to the back of a chair promotes closer understanding and attention – like Piggy in 'Lord of the Flies' whose damaged glasses symbolised damage done to him as a person.

Topic – 'The Healthy Eater Restaurant' [Key-Stage 2]

In order to play the game that we are going to describe your class and you have to learn all about healthy ingredients of restaurant dishes (a big planning and learning stage). You and your class will make labels for individual ingredients drawn from many different categories of food (proteins, fats, starch) with an indication of the nourishment value under each name. Now the fun starts:

Invite each member of your class to 'become' an ingredient [wearing the label or tabard] standing on the larder or refrigerator shelf of the 'Healthy Eater Restaurant'. You are now going to adopt the role of a care-free, obsessive, stupid chef [hefty hat!] who talks his/her way through the cooking, seizing inappropriate ingredients and measures for what s/he is making. The ingredients' responsibility is to shout 'STOP!' and correct the chef, pointing out the error of his/her ways as s/he works – and literally pointing to the menus that your class have already made in preparation for the game, now displayed outside the 'restaurant'. S/he is none too pleased with the ingredients' advice and tries, often in underhand ways, to ignore it, but the ingredients persist. When the game is over, you all go over the mistakes the chef made – and, if you like, give him/her a test to see whether anything has gone home! Other hygiene matters such as chef's avoidance of washing hands, dropping things on floor and using same spoon for everything can be inserted as seems suitable.

In this chapter we have given a variety of examples of different kinds of role play, each bearing in mind the single question of 'How far can we challenge and at the same time protect?' We hope we have demonstrated how our examples follow the dimensions of 'Accessibility', 'Investment', 'Facilities', 'Responsibility', 'Form', 'Planning' and 'Reflection'.

Reference

1. Tattum, Delwyn and Herbert, Graham (1993) *Countering Bullying* Stoke on Trent: Trentham Books, pp.151-160.

CHAPTER FOUR
SIGN IN ROLE-PLAY

A **definition of Sign**: Those aspects of the total environment from which a 'reader' seeks to make a coherent meaning of the situation and circumstance.

Signs only come into being when there is someone who wants to read them. Setting up a role-play demands careful and imaginative selection of those signs your class is likely to respond to. Conan Doyle's detective will serve us well with an illustration; of effective 'sign reading':

...it would be difficult to name any articles which afford a fitter field for inference than a pair of glasses, especially so remarkable a pair as these. That they belong to a woman I infer from their delicacy, and also, of course [the owner] being a person of refinement and well dressed. They are, as you perceive, handsomely mounted in solid gold, and it is inconceivable that anyone who wore such glasses could be slatternly in other respects. You will find that the clips are too wide for your nose, showing that the lady's nose is very broad at the base... you will perceive, Watson, that the glasses are concave and of unusual strength. A lady whose vision has been extremely contracted all her life...' and so on.[1]

Sherlock Holmes, speaking personally, has selected one element from all the circumstances of 'sign' which surrounded him. Because his 'point of view' is that of a detective, he will at that moment of 'reading' the elegant spectacles apply that particular brand of 'productive bias'. Had he been in the frame of mind to approach his task as an optician, his productive bias would have introduced other meanings such as: 'There must be somewhere a lady with myopic vision, missing her glasses... these spectacles allow me to assess the condition of the owner's eyesight.' Likewise a jeweller , a pawn-broker or a student of phrenology could all 'read' the spectacles for meanings relevant to their 'frame of mind' or 'point of view', an expression we have already used in Chapter 3 in connection with how your class are expected to function in the role-play.

Thus, if you were setting up a role-play about Sherlock Holmes, you would not only need, by the careful selection of signs, to arrest your students' attention to Holmes' 'context', you would also want them to understand Holmes' 'point of view', that is, how he sees his world and why he chooses to see his world this way – his 'motivating purpose'. Put another way, one can say the fiction embraces two aspects, the **identification with the context and identification with the role's point of view**. You will find that whereas most of your classes will identify with the former, the latter has to be 'won'. They may readily grasp the context, but can they identify with the characters' *motivating purpose* in doing what they do? If they are going to take on the role of those characters, it is not enough to simulate the characters' actions – they must grasp the motivation behind them. A clear example of what we mean is in Chapter 1 (A6a) on Road Safety when children are dealing with the aftermath of a friend's death in a traffic accident. The 'context' of the work is a missing friend. The 'point of view' is doing something to help a relative realise that friends want to say 'sorry' – in this case preparing sympathy cards and taking them round to the house. Now the work can only have credibility if your class can be lured into making and taking those cards because *to them, as they develop their fictional point of view*, it seems the right thing to do. They must genuinely accept the need to write and take them; otherwise it will be an empty exercise. **Sign** is one of the means of achieving this. Let us re-examine the episode of visiting the relative in her home. The Role-play instructions were:

A6a ... After creating the wall map with its marked lamp-post and flowers, you can build up with your class how they want you to represent a bereaved family member – they help you decide what relation they want you to be; they discuss how you are feeling; they define a space in the classroom as 'your house'; they decide what you are in the middle of doing when you arrive; they decide where the front door is – and you supply a piece of cardboard on which you draw a knocker or bell. The children call at the door, you invite them in and they show you all the cards they have brought – you can hand round milk and biscuits, if you wish!, for the visit has to be long enough for them to gather something of your feeling of loss and how you are managing.

If you can capture the interest of your class in creating *your* role, they have a chance of building a vested interest in relating to it. They are virtually selecting the appropriate 'signs', in keeping with the context and with what they are beginning to sense is the appropriate 'point of view'. If you feel they are not ready to cooperate to this extent, then you could build that space and impose the signs – as they make their cards, the 'visual' sign of the inanimate front door; the 'movement' sign of your action as you busy yourself in the house or slowly pack a box of toys or just sit perfectly still 'remembering'. Your 'signing' should lure them into wanting to deliver their cards – because it seems the right thing to do.

Different kinds of signing

The 'Signs' you use to help your class believe in a fictional character or place tend to function in three different ways – (1) as representations (2) as indicators and (3) as lures. Let's illustrate these by re-examining a previous exercise. In our section on Health Education we included a 'School Dinners' theme for infants which read as follows (p.76):

This involves a classroom table covered with white drawing paper on which you draw the outline of big serving dishes, blank labels for each child and labels for the dishes. Your class draw or stick pictures of their choices of food into the dish outlines while you give each dish a name: e.g. potatoes – baked; fish – fried; fish – baked; etc. You fill in their blank labels with the right words as each child decides on the kind of food s/he likes for school lunch. In role as the 'dinner lady' you invite them to 'queue up' for their food [you've given them paper plates] which you serve from the appropriate dish – with real serving spoons. Back in their seats they draw their choice of food onto their plates. All are displayed. You and children then make a graph or bar chart of 'food choice'.

Brief as this exercise is it has acquired some interesting signs. The drawings you make of food dishes on a counter are clearly functioning as representations. So why did you not choose to have *real* serving dishes? It is a fascinating aspect of role-play that the representation can be more authentic than the real. One answer to the paradox is that the more real the dishes are the more real is their *emptiness!* and, logically, the less truthful is the fiction. So, the words MASHED POTATOES on a label ['indicators'] below the dish drawing and the drawing itself, together with the way you as 'dinner lady' treat the representation, create sufficient authenticity. The question then arises, should you have real serving spoons or simply mime them? Does not *their* (i.e. the spoons') reality in turn emphasise the unreality of food being there? To a degree it may, but this is outweighed by other factors. The spoon will have the additional function of confirming you as a dinner lady – it represents your badge of office; it stands for your authority over food and over queues of little people who have to 'take their turn'. And your *visible* steady movement of the spoon from dish to plate, accompanied by your naming [and thereby respecting] and commenting on each individual's choice of food is a necessary part of the ritual. And, this is part of a project on Health Education and the hygienic switch of spoons from dish to dish has to be *seen* – but you're going to try not to let your spoons touch 'the bottom of the dishes' – the inauthentic sound of the edge of a spoon on paper may ruin everything! So, we have the covered table that acts as a *representational* sign, standing in for a serving hatch, we have labels as *indicating* signs of food dishes. It is, however, the inviting gesture from the dinner-lady/teacher handing out 'full plates' that *lures*. The luring sign 'catches' the receiver – like a handshake! If someone unexpectedly offers you a hand to shake you are 'caught' by this sudden sign of comradeship – you are *lured* into handshaking! It is the same in role-play; the teacher's role must at some point 'catch' your class into participating.

Thus we are in an exciting area of choice, carefully balancing one priority over another. The aim is economy and coherence. But how do you decide? It is a matter of inner logic. The curriculum project is 'Noticing food' – *what food looks and tastes like*, its shape on the plate, its texture. Every step of the project must focus onto this objective. Hence, the 'sign' of the 'empty plate waiting to be filled', becomes the material on which coloured crayons create the carefully selected and much discussed food. A teacher might mistakenly assume that merely enacting a 'pretend' school dinner might be a way of introducing the topic of food – but it has no logical centre – such an exercise could go in too many directions, diffused by its lack of focus.

But the representational and the indicating signs are not enough on their own. The children must have power over their own role-play, so your signing must **empower** them and, further, **lure** them into how they are to function in sharing the role-play 'game'. Let's look at two contrasted ways of introducing the above exercise.

Situation 1

When children have drawn or glued pictures of their chosen food into the outline of the big serving dishes, you say:

> *'Shall we use these paper plates... then you can come to lunch and I'll use this spoon... and ... so when you come to the food counter... after you've washed your hands, of course... I'll give you some... and you pretend to put it on your plates'*

Such an invitation is perfectly reasonable. It directs the class towards what is going to happen and tells them the order of events that will follow in the sequence you require. It 'keys' them into the context and the actions. So they will do it as a class going along with teacher's ideas. But it needs more to help them feel they are there. There is little empowerment; they are not *lured* into 'being there' along with the 'dinner lady'.

Alternative Situation 2

When they have completed drawing or sticking pictures, you:

(Sign 1) from among the class, survey the dishes, making 'teacher' kind of comments

(Sign 2) changing to *'Well... what a nice dinner counter the school children will find... when they come in to collect their lunch... I bet the food today is just what they all like...'* [today! and there are some characters called school children – and their arrival is imminent!]

(Sign 3) Looking at your watch... *'Goodness me... I'd better get the plates ready...'* [not a 'teacher' thing to say! and you're bustling with the plates!]

(Sign 4) Raising your voice a little as you lay out spoons: *'Can you all wash your hands... I've put all new soap tablets in just this morning'* [So **we** are those school children about to have dinner! help! what do we do???!!!]

(Sign 5) Just a nod in the direction of the 'washbasins' and *'...then come and collect a plate...'*

(Sign 6) You take up spoon and signal 'Waiting' by gesture and a glance along the food.

(Sign 7 – if they are still hesitating) You lift up a plate and wait for it to be taken – which it will!

From then onwards, all during the serving, if you feel confident that the children are enjoying 'the game' and play along with relevant behaviour, you will keep stressing 'now time', and continue to 'empower' them – they control your spoons and you!

It is worth examining the above version, especially the carefully chosen dialogue by the teacher-in-role. Among all the signs, there are two that do more than create the 'context', important as that is. You drop in a reference that keys your class into *who* they are going to be and what they are going to be required to do: *'Well... what a nice dinner counter the school children will find... when they come in to collect their lunch...'* Thus they *hear* that when the 'game starts they are to be schoolchildren queueing up for lunch' They *hear* this, but it is not in itself empowering, It importantly **keys** them into the game, in the sense that they now know their role, but this is but intellectual recognition. Neverthess, they will also perceive that you are already playing the game of 'being there': *'Goodness me... I'd better get the plates ready...'* Still needed, however, if there is to be any kind of action and your class are going to feel included in your 'game', is the **lure** of your taking up the spoon and offering a plate **to be taken off you** (like the offered hand to be shaken!). 'Lure' is mostly an impulse to respond to teacher-in-role's remark, question and/or gesture, but occasionally a verbal sign can lure. An arrow that reads: **THIS WAY TO THE TREASURE** is an obvious example!

Now is your opportunity to introduce all the curriculum dimensions you want to follow in the syllabus on food and eating. So your chatter, in a suitable 'restricted' code of language, will be about names, quantities, colours, tastes and textures. It does not matter that you may *seem* to get more turns at talking than they get, because you will give away power by deferring to whatever they ask for. Your kind of talking will always be as if you are 'opening up' a point, needing a complementary response but never sounding like teacher asking questions. '*I bet you like a lot... say 'when'...*' and always look for the opportunity to expand concepts. To the child who asks for 'meat', pointing to your dishes you might ask, '*Now would that be 'chicken' or 'beef'?...chicken..O.K... nice slice of breast we have here...*'

Are you really 'empowering'?

Sometimes you will *think* you have empowered your class, but you are deceiving yourself. Let's look at another infant example we have already described A9 (p.8). It read as follows:

A9. You address the class as if they are adults: *I've heard that your firm is good at making posters that appeal to young children. I work for — — Council and we're worried about the number of road accidents lately. It's five year olds* [the fictitious age chosen always younger than the actual age of the participants] *we're most worried about – there was an accident outside a school last week, a child was waiting for a parent who was a bit late turning up... They don't seem to understand the dangers the way older children do. Do you think you could do some posters for the council that would help these children understand...?* Each child with crayons and paper creates an 'accident' poster. As they work you go round stimulating individual children to tell you the meaning of the drawing.

It sounds such a good idea to treat your class as 'experts' and ask their help. But let's think about it. What the teacher in this exercise does is, by assuming the role of spokesperson for the Council, *verbally* endow the class with a role – that they are adults; that they are adults, belonging to a firm; and that they are good at posters. If you use no other signs than your words, the class will get the message, but at that point they will neither belong to a specialist firm nor be designers of posters – and they will be **dis**empowered. Your words seem to require adult behaviour and, unconsciously, they will register that instruction, but that does not key them into thinking expertly. They will not feel that *their* thinking can have influence.

So which forms of sign might you use that would empower an expert's response? The 'long' route' would be for you gradually to build up a fictional context in which they are a firm of expert designers (using a whole range of signs in order to do this) and when that fiction is well-established, they would be ready *in their adult role* to design the posters. But in this book we are mostly concerned with short-term role-play, where there is no time or inclination to lay down a full-scale 'Mantle of the Expert' approach, in which case you would be advised to use the expertise *they already have*: an ability to see things through a child's eye.

So which forms of sign might you use which 'keys' an expert's response without making advanced preparations? If you borrow the 'Lollipop person's' props – a yellow coat, hat and tightly wound scarf [a 'representative' sign] and a lollipop [or even just a label: School Crossing Person [an indicative sign] and a makeshift lollipop might suffice] – and start a dialogue that begins [perhaps with a voice and a speaking style that 'isn't quite yours]: '*Before I let you cross the road, could I ask you a favour...*?' [Notice how '*before I let you cross the road...*' keys your class into knowing who they are to be and what they are expected to do, whereas '*...could I ask you a favour?...*' lures them into participating] and you go on to talk about a recent accident to a child outside school... and how you work for the Council... and the Council don't always know what to do for the best... but you wondered... you had an idea.. *children* know what other children need to know... and if they were to send posters to the Council... they could help other children be careful in crossing the road...etc . And then, of course, you come out of role, and listen as their teacher to what the lollipop person has suggested, shifting your tense from 'now time' to the past – 'What did the lollipop lady say?'

Now you have empowered them, for they are the ones who *know* what makes things go wrong when children have to cross roads. And the signs are interesting, visual as well as verbal, with a strong sense of being part of an interrupted flow of now time [...before I let you cross the road...] It is a sense of fictional *place* as well as time that initiates participants into *sensing* as well knowing who they are. The lollipop is three dimensional occupying a physical place, the coat is yellow glaringly present, the lollipop person is doing a job – in time and *space* – and it is easier for your class to share fictional place than to share the kind of fictional *instruction* of the exercise (A9) above. In that exercise your role remained 'spaceless' and 'placeless', an abstraction from the Council, and your talk simply extended that abstraction.

If we look at A1 (Chapter 1) we find a classic signing of place. It read:

A1. You may give your class some practical exercises in Road Drill by inviting them to agree that the line drawn in the hall is a pavement edge at which they are required to 'look left'. 'look right' and 'left again' – having heard you talk of the dangers of *not* following the procedure.

and although we pointed out that, standing alone, such simulation is limited in learning potential, it serves adequately in terms of establishing for the class where they are and what is going on. Here we sign a definition of *territory* economically – a simple line marked on the hall floor to *represent* a pavement edge. Note that it *must* be a fixed line – sticky tape – for string, though representing straightness and indicating where the edge is, cannot symbolise the immovability of a pavement edge – fixed and underfoot. In preparing 'signs' you will continually be weighing up choices and you could unintentionally reduce credibility by signing the wrong or inadequate meaning, as in this case, giving the wrong 'feel' relating to 'standing at the pavement edge'. Even here you are conscious that an important aspect is still missing – the critical feeling of 'stepping off' the pavement. This representation is unlikely to be achievable, so as you conduct the exercise you will try to compensate by building the image of 'waiting at the edge... and then... looking left, looking right... taking the decisive step'. Still not sufficient, but you will have done your best by *modelling* the action of looking and then 'stepping' onto the road.

But supposing you want, not a pavement edge, but a demarcation sign which has a chance to act a temporary *barrier*, say, an area of a road-works site marked off with stretched plastic and a sign: Danger Keep Out or even No Entry. Now a fixed line on the floor becomes inappropriate for the stretched plastic, or whatever you use to represent it functions both as a barrier sign and a removable *right of passage* sign – and is replaceable. Thus in selecting 'place' sign you have to anticipate the kinds of action that will be involved.

Signing an historical figure – Adolescents (not in role) studying Shakespeare

You may need to sign more elaborately. You may want to represent a life-style such as a portrait or a particular person's territory, a territory not yet owned by the class, which has been set aside by you, waiting to be acknowledged and entered. It may at first seem a formidable task without, say, the proper period objects or the means creating an unfamiliar environment inside a classroom space. Don't give up! The first rule is rigorously to limit what you use.

Let us take the idea of a place being given *sign*ificance, so that it becomes a room belonging to a person relevant to the school curriculum (Galileo, Shakespeare, Darwin, Elizabeth Gaskell, a Bronte sister, Lister, Scott of the Antarctic and so on). First you must sign the border where class territory and role territory meet – usually a cloth spread on the floor can suggest the 'no-go' area. Older classes will respect this. Smaller children may need actual barriers at first, a low bench, say, as an indicator. The 'space and territory' established, you can build the signs of occupation and professional interests within it.

What you select now depends entirely on how, in the light of the curriculum, you visualise the 'place' being seen by your students as demanding a visit. Let us consider how different educational contexts require different arrangements of the 'evidence', for this use of a special place is always going to set the students in a frame of 'inspecting' something. Let us suppose that studying a Shakespeare play is your context and you want the text and Shakespeare's intention to be central to the work.

Usually classes expect teachers to be the source of knowledge, but in our work the text will be the primary source. Displaying the text will be your priority and, secondly, you must highlight a selected focus to be borne in mind as they meet the text. Thirdly, it must seem reasonable and indeed necessary to enter the 'place', in this case, 'Shakespeare's room'.

Let us assume that the text to be studied is *Antony and Cleopatra* and that the chosen focus is the apparent deterioration of Anthony: What led to his final '*I am dying, Egypt, dying*'?

Your first session is going to be a session for studying the text. This is conventional teaching, in that no-one is going to be in a fictional role. But there are key differences. Before your class arrive you will plan your classroom, selecting which corner is going to be 'Shakespeare's room' marked by a length of cloth on the floor. Round the rest of the classroom you will have 'laid out' the text, either separate sheets round the walls or on the floor [there's nothing like feeling in control of a text that you look down on!] and bearing your focus in mind, you have made reading easier by using colour coded underlining of all characters throughout the unfamiliar text. You divide the class into groups and hand each group a card, again colour coded, with statements and questions on them, such as 'Is there evidence regarding why Anthony took Octavia to wife whilst still involved with Cleopatra?' [Do you see the difference in sign between a student reading 'took Octavia to wife' and simply 'married Octavia'?]

What these scripts spread round the room sign from the moment your students enter controls the whole study enterprise. Normally, students have individual bound texts, signalling individual, 'bookbound' study in a private space. A spread-out text signs collaboration and a 'game of searching'. Another difference is your non-authoritative signing. The way you hand out the cards and refer to the questions on them will carry a kind of *deferring* to the text, even if no more than a nod in its direction. But there is more than that. There is 'the room', with its cloth to show the area, a covered table, a chair or stool with a hat or cloak thrown over it [hat need only be a velvet cushion cover], a quill pen and ink, and an unlit candle in a candle stick. And you will *say* nothing about it during this study period, but you will have 'signed' your awareness of it with your occasional glances in its direction. Its presence, unspoken of but signed, is a *promise*. Against this hint of things to come, you check whether the groups are finding some kind of answers from the 'evidence' – and if they are not, you might vaguely wonder whether there is anything that could help them in that scene when... but you're not sure. You wonder... *what he had in mind when he said...* You suppose... he must have had some understanding of Roman history and Egypt.

Shakespeare comes in – the next session

No, he doesn't 'come in'. It's easier for you and the role-player to handle if s/he (men and women are interchangeable in these circumstances – they are only 'demonstrating') is already there in his own 'room' which they saw but did not examine in their previous lesson. So it may be that you gather your class outside the classroom and help them anticipate that entering this time is going to be special. They will discover the space occupied – 'Shakespeare' sitting with the quill in his fingers [and if they've seen the film *Shakespeare in Love*, they'll expect inky fingers!] and the candle lit, finishing a play. And as they stand and stare they may realise that as he mutters it to himself it is *their* play, *Anthony and Cleopatra*.

You may be wondering where this extra person in the classroom can be found. If you are lucky, you may have a colleague in the English department with a free period or you have a student on a long school practice. Otherwise you will have to play the part yourself signing Shakespeare, signing teacher, signing Shakespeare/teacher.

If you do not have a helper, then you will need to make a contract, saying something like, '*Will you agree that when I sit at that table... light that candle... take up that quill... that I can represent working on the text of* Anthony and Cleopatra?' And you don't even need to don cuffs or a ruff; to do so hinders smooth movement into your teacher function when necessary.

Now let us see how your students, through a visit to this 'room' can continue to study the text without loss of power. First they should have time to 'read' the room, watch the role working on the text and, *importantly*, enjoy knowing that it is contrived. If you are playing the role, after a suitable 'taking it in' time, you might make a statement, such as '*I bid you welcome. Do you seek Will Shakespeare?*' [using a style of language that is vaguely 'not modern'] – and of course they do! But if another person is taking the role, you have much more scope, for instance, discussing with the class how they can interrupt his work on the final lines of the play. And it is your *students* who must take it upon themselves to address the role. This moment is crucial. It implies an agreement to play along with the fiction, to play the game. If *you* do it, it remains your fiction, your game.

Neither you nor the role must convey that you know more than your students – they will be easily disempowered. You can have a text in slender book form at hand, as if you are their quick 'looker up' of particular references, which can then be confirmed by a nod in the direction of the 'wall' text which is still there as *their* evidence. They will also have their cards from the previous lesson and their group conclusions about, say, Anthony's deterioration. And it is these previous 'findings' that must become a springboard into engaging with the role. Whichever student becomes the first spokesperson for the class is required to select from scribbled notes from the previous lesson and translate them into the form of a question that has to sound right in addressing the author. A formidable task – and yet you must not *model* it. It may be that you will know your class well enough to realise they need some practice at the end of the first lesson in turning their 'findings' into a question form, so that you have already said: '...*that bit you've written there about Anthony making a daft decision... how would we ask him about it... if we had him here now... what exactly would we ask him...?*'

Once that first question has been voiced to the role, *your* function where necessary is to quickly scan your compact text and nodding to the larger textual display, saying things such as, '*We mean the bit when...*' and the role's function is also to refer to that text as though the students are helping him *recall* it, so statements like '*I seem to think... at the time... I wanted people to realise... (or know about, or worry about etc.)...*' Verbal sign operates here. 'Seem' is a hesitant word followed by informed evidence. For example, referring to Anthony's agreement to fight by sea when all his skills and experience lay in land wars, the role may say something like: '*I* think *Anthony did not know that Cleopatra's ships were quite unseaworthy, but I was* sure *he was so tangled up with Egypt at that time that he could take the risk – even if the experienced general in him had some misgivings... certainly his troops had!*' Thus a process unfolds of his notions being set alongside theirs as a further stimulus to textual study.

Studying Shakespearean Theatre architecture – adolescents in role

If we take a different context, say, a Theatre Studies class considering how a theatre of Shakepeare's time would be used during a performance, different kinds of signs would be involved and the meanings would be discovered by the class quite differently.

Instead of the starting point being a study of a 'wall' text, the initiation into the work could now be 'preparing to be guides around the replica built in London in 1996 of the original Globe Theatre, advising tourists (and students of the theatre!) on historical usage'. Alternatively, again needing the text, they could work in the context of T.I.E. actors who are going to tour a set of examination plays to schools and they need to work out how their play will be performed as in the Globe or Swan theatres. In both cases they must have access to accurate theatre designs of a Bank-side theatre, with architects' notes attached referring to descending and ascending features (potential graves and balconies) and those designs will need to be on display in a fictional environment representing some back-stage space such as a rehearsal room.

Let us concentrate on the first of these, the 'guides'. As for the work on *Anthony and Cleopatra* we suggest the first session should be based on student enquiry, this time to study the drawings instead of the text. Small groups can again, stimulated by questions devised by you on cards, search for answers on the wall or on a long table or on the floor. You collect opinions, inferences and suggestions from the groups. But this time, you and they will be in role from the beginning.

A 'guide's way-in to Theatre design

You can use your role either to establish that they are already guides, spared from a museum, or better, that they have applied to train as guides and are looking for a job in Sam Wanamaker's new Globe theatre – not yet finished but house staff are being appointed and it is your job as house manager to appoint or train guides as there is going to be a rush of tourists with an unusual degree of scholarly interest.

If you want to establish they are already guides then the keying by you must include reference to their past experience and your welcome '*Did you manage to get in the car park... I told the attendant the new guides would be starting today...*' will lure them into participation – reinforced by your handing out PERMITS [with space for signatures and a fastening]

But if you want them to be arriving to *train* as guides, then you have to convey that you don't know anything about that 'scholarship stuff' – you're a manager not a scholar, but you assume the applicants can 'mug it up' before it opens in a few months time '*Mind, they'll have to get a move on... we're supposed to be open to the public in three months... the builders can't let us wander round... but I've got these plans from the architect... they're only copies... so you can write on them if you have to... this'll be your common room, by the way... it'll have a notice on the door... but you're lucky to have the room... the actors can't get in the theatre yet to rehearse... you better wear these badges by the way else someone will want to know what you're doing here... there's coffee over there...*' They can only have artists' impressions, architect's plans and photographs, so you will have to convey that they are not allowed to enter the stage area of the new structure yet, to have a look at it.

Thus you have to 'win' your class to the idea of having to learn a job – and of being on show when they do it. *This* becomes the focus of your attention, *not* whether they have an urgent interest in theatre architecture of Shakespeare's times. So the work will proceed through a series of **tasks**, each linked with requirements of the *job*. All your initial signing will be businesslike and 'cool'. You will have already added comments or labels to parts of the drawings on display, indicating accurate information about the placings and measurements [modern, of course] of trapdoors for 'ghosts and 'gravediggers' – sufficient of these to grab the attention of the class when they do their first browsing. It is while they are browsing that you verbally build background information that they are going to need... *'...they must have had good timbers to support all those balconies and storeys... we're on the fourth floor up here!... they seem to think this building'll be the nearest there's ever been to an accurate replica of the Globe...'*

It can be assumed that the theatre will have a display area, helping people learn about how the theatre was used and that the 'guides' are to be responsible for creating the display. At the centre could be a paper representation of Shakespeare (copied from portraits, using sugar paper) round which the guides could stick extracts from plays, selected for their specific theatre location. Thus their tasks are a mixture of practising explaining their newly acquired knowledge and presenting relevant writing on a wall display. They could make a paper three dimensional model of the new Globe to be placed at the side of the wall display.

In summary, your work will include the following tasks:

1. You give them 'guide' status – badges; drawn coat pegs with trainees' names; drawn coffee-pot.

2. Studying the architect's plans, photographs etc – and which are the parts that will have to be explained

3. Beginning a wall display, including making a life-size paper figure of Shakespeare.

4. Make a 3D model of The Globe (as it will look when building is complete)

5. Finding bits of text relating to staging – you can have '*come across some...*' 'This wooden O' might be a good start and onto scenes with graves, balconies and tombs as a further lure and you hope that from them they move onto how Shakespeare might have got his effects of ships, streets and forests. And they may notice that his words sometimes paint the scene.

6. Placing selected texts round the portrait.

7. Planning and practising the guides presentations and should you and they wish...

8. Take one play (the relevant examination text, of course) and prepare a wall display of where each scene would be acted on the Shakespearean stage.

[Note: the above numbers do not represent discrete phases of work – there will be an overlap of activities and sometimes they will run concurrently, with different groups tackling, say, the Shakespeare cut-out, while others are searching texts for graves.]

There is a **coherence** to the above activities because they sustain the same point of view and context – guides, guides learning to teach less informed people than themselves. This exercise is a good example of harnessing your class' reluctance to study Shakespearean texts by inviting them to play a role also disinclined to make the text central – 'positive disinclination!'.

Coherence refers simultaneously to the dramatic and the epistemological. It is achieved along each of these artistic and educational dimensions by retaining the same fictional context, the same point of view in relation to the fiction and the same order of 'sign'. It is as if the way into the fiction dictates how the knowledge is to be opened up. As we have seen, if the knowledge is 'spectacles', it tells us very little until we know that it is Sherlock Holmes who is doing the looking; if the knowledge is *Anthony and Cleopatra*, it tells us very little until we know that it is to be opened up by students meeting William Shakespeare; if the knowledge is theatre architecture, it tells us very little until we know that it is to be opened up by theatre 'guides'. Likewise, if your class are studying the story of The Nativity, we remain in the dark until we know that it is to be opened up by but *one prevailing point of view*, say, all the characters are preparing for the Roman Census, whereas another class might be opening it up through T.S. Eliot's *Journey of the Magi*. In the Road Safety example mentioned earlier, the subject of grieving was opened up for young children through the making, giving and receiving of condolence cards.

In each instance the 'signing' of the fiction should contribute to that coherence. Let us think our way through finding the right signs for *Journey of the Magi*. This poem is a 'recollection' of a past significant event. A narrator simply says 'We returned to our places, these kingdoms' Making a 'place' is much more than representing a room. You are making significant territory which is *more* than itself. It is simultaneously itself and what it *stands for*. It is 'out of time'; in a 'different time'. It is only to be seen from afar; or sometimes it can be entered, – if you follow the code; Its characters can emerge, but only if we and they follow the code. Its characters may speak but we have to learn the proper style of language. And the characters can only know what their medium of art or history allows them to know.

Chamber Theatre

'Chamber theatre' is a useful genre to illustrate precision of signing. Let us conclude this chapter by using the text of Eliot's poem, *Journey of the Magi*, as if planning to interpret it through Chamber Theatre. The 'coherence law' here is never to muddle different uses of sign. The most economical sign of astrologers can be a paper window (eastern design!) showing a number of stars and paper shadows on a wall of their instruments. They wear eastern robes of 'kings' as traditionally shown in paintings. They may sit on cushions, perusing their scrolls. The 'room' with its eastern-style window is not a specific place, for the three kings, having returned to their separate kingdoms, are sharing one story, one 'dis-ease'. If we were to extend these images into 'Chamber Theatre', we would have to consider a rationale for using this kind of elaborate treatment. The following points might persuade you:

1. Magi are recalling and reliving past events, until, suddenly, for the last 12 lines of the poem we are in the present.

2. They are telling their history to an *audience*.

3. Their story has three kinds of information: places, terrain and climate and their behaviour or, to put it another way, what they saw, what they suffered and what they understood (or failed to).

4. Their recollections reflect perturbation that nothing is resolved.

5. They share a consensus view of events past and present attitudes, and only on three occasions refer to 'I' and these seem inclusive by inference.

Journey of the Magi

The script could be as follows:

The Characters

There are 3 speaking, moving Magi

There is an artist/scribe who 'sets all down'

There is a Female servant

There are 3, identically clothed Magi, 'dream figures, memories of themselves

There is another group of 'dream figures' who represent situations as they are remembered and provide, as a chorus, the 'sounds' that are heard.

The 3 Magi (in the present) are seated on cushions behind low tables on which their scrolls rest and are used as aides memoirs as they speak of the events. They sit side by side.

The dream figures are seated to one side, dressed drably so they may represent different kinds of servants, camel men, hostility etc. There lie 3 bundles of firewood, long enough to be carried across shoulders and arms of 3 dream figures (a broom stick handle with leaves and sticks fastened on them is sufficient

There is a hidden blue shawl for Mary, lantern for Joseph and doll child to be used when needed.

The dream Magi carry a gift which they never relinquish.

The Play

Stillness over all

The artist stands with easel and long scroll of paper which will drop as more and more drawing is revealed. The drawing will be made in advance so that as words are spoken, and dream figures demonstrate events as they are told of, the artist demonstrates painting at high speed and with energy, as he watches dream events.

The female servant stands at a distance with tray of sherbet goblets beside her. Her back is to the Magi before she serves them and after-wards.

The action begins: three Magi move their hands and start to open their individual scrolls (on which Eliot's text can be written)

At this gesture the artist takes up scroll and lays on the easel, taking up brush and palette.

The three Magi look at each other and one says the first line of poem: 'A cold coming...'

Simultaneously, dream Magi begin to move against the elements, guarding their gifts.

The artist watches them and paints as if they are the models.

The three present Magi watch dream Magi and continue speaking the next four lines to 'the very dead of winter".

This part of painted scroll starts to fall down and so that painting can be seen by audience. Artist 'draws in' some landscape.

One present Magi speaks 'There were times we regretted' and ela-borate slowly, in turn, 'the summer palaces, slopes, terraces', as if each one is reminding others...

Artist paints these as 'dream' landscape...

And 'dream' Magi lie down

Servant moves forward with the sherbet and this 'reminds' present Magi of the next line, '*And the silken girls bring sherbet*'

Artist paints dream images above sleeping Kings and scroll falls down to reveal picture.

Servant girls withdraws and waits at back again.

Dream Magi are rudely awakened by Camel men (enacted by dream group), kicking camels. demanding money, drinking liquor and catching women. **During this, present Magi speak relevant lines (correctly spaced).**

Artist paints. Scroll falls down to reveal hostile images.

'*A hard time we had of it*' – spoken by one present Magi, as dream Magi are now alone, protecting their gifts., struggle forward. As 'voices' line is spoken they are assailed by dream voices... *folly... folly... folly...* dying away.

'*Then at dawn...* ' present Magi speaks with new '*energy*'

Artist paints; dream Magi stand and gaze and then move slowly forward, a 'chorus' making sound of turning wheel ('beating') – it grows louder as Magi 'walk on spot' until it is loud around them. Then 3 of the dream figures rise holding branches across their shoulders as if carrying firewood and are resting for a moment – the centred branched figure being taller. Sound of galloping hooves in the distance as they stand...

The present Magi speak: '
And three trees on the low sky

Horse hooves louder, then dying into distance as dream Magi watch 'trees'. As hooves die away:

'And an old white horse galloped away in the meadow" – and branched figures move into crowd and lower branches.

Artist paints; scroll drops

Present Magi speak of 'tavern' and 'lintel' – dream group create crowded tavern – dicing, begging, kicking, and, above all, noticing 'gifts' carried by the dream kings.

After 'wine skins', dream Magi point to heavens, and look around... crowd puzzled, drifting away.

'*But there was no information, so we continued" is spoken by present Magi as dream Magi 'walk'.*

As they walk, a dream group appear as Mary, Joseph and the baby. Joseph sees the dream Magi and beckons them with lantern

The present Magi divide the lines:

'*And arrived at evening*
Not a moment too soon
Finding the place"

They are as still as in a painting

The artist paints on scroll

Dream Magi consult, examine 'star' above and finally decide they will leave gifts and so place them.

'It was (you may say) satisfactory' is spoken as **the dream Magi leave**.

Artist paints, scroll falls down, **and the three present Magi rise slowly and one at a time replace the three dream Magi watching a now 'frozen' family group.**

The next lines are divided:

'All this was a long time ago, I remember
And I would do it again, but set down
This set down
This"

The one who says *'Set down...'* moves over to artist, directing him to write...

For *'This set down... This'* a second Magi comes over to artist while a third goes over to the window, ready for:

'Were we led all that way for
Birth or Death?'...spoken slowly so that artist can write it down

1st Magi moves over to frozen Mary/Joseph group: *'There was a birth certainly'* as he looks carefully

2nd Magi: *'We had evidence' also looks carefully'*

3rd Magi: *'And no doubt' also moves and looks carefully...*

All three present Magi stand near dream nativity group in the classic pose of Kings at nativity in portraits.

The artist writes

The Magi speak the next lines deeply troubled:

1st Magi, moving over to the window:
'I had seen birth and death,
But had thought they were different;

2nd and 3rd Magi, staying, peering closely at nativity:
'...this Birth was
hard and bitter agony for us...'

1st Magi, from window:
'...like Death, our Death.' He slowly sheds the rich garment and is seen to be wearing a simple garment. The others do the same as they return to their cushions with, a line in turn:

'We returned to our places, These kingdoms,
But no longer at ease here, in the old dispensation"

Magi at window, looking out: 'with an alien people clutching their gods' he moves slowly to stand between the other two:

'I shall be glad of another death"

They look towards the nativity which slowly rises and stands powerfully

Artist completes writing – sees them standing and quietly departs leaving paintings.

Magi reseat themselves and study their own scrolls in silence.

The nativity group quietly move away...

Reference

1 *The Penguin Complete Sherlock Holmes* by Sir Arthur Conan Doyle London: Penguin 1982

CHAPTER FIVE

WHO ARE YOU TEACHING?

This chapter is about finding an appropriate relationship with the group you are working with. It will be necessary to introduce the idea of the participants' *cultural role*, and the tutor's *social* role, roles identifiable in addition to any fictional role that either side might play. If we look back through the book, asking the bald question of this chapter's title, 'Who are you teaching?', we could list the various groups as 'Primary School children learning about road safety or health education; upper adolescents learning about disloyalty; *Anthony and Cleopatra* or Shakespearean theatre architecture; trainee gas-fitters learning to anticipate problems related to house visits; medical students looking at a doctor's working day; Northern Gas managers testing their team skills; and nurses learning to be ward managers. For some practitioners in the use of role-play, especially those whose approach is derived from simulation exercises, it is enough to know who the 'target' group are and what the 'target' learning is. They can straightforwardly arrange a series of problems for the participants to solve and a subsequent debriefing that promotes reflection n what took place. But of course seeing your class as a *target* grou is to endow them with a cultural role. That is how you see them   d that is **who they will be**. Their cultural make-up will also be i luenced by the disposition they bring to *learning and role-play ii ʒeneral, and* to *the topic in particular –* and even *you* will be part   their perception! Thus 'who they are' will largely depend on a blend of the attitude they bring and how you choose to perceive them.

In most educational contexts there is a tacit agreement that your class will be framed as 'students' and that you will behave as a 'leader/tutor/teacher'. Thus their cultural identity depends on this traditional imbalanced, two-sided relationship of teacher/pupils, tutor/students, trainer/trainees. We suggest, however, that within that context there is potentially such a qualitatively significant range of *modes* of tutor/student relationships that no bland assumptions can be made. One cannot arrange a series of problems for the participants to solve through role-play without first knowing which relationship you and they are going to be in, that is, which kind of tutor/student roles outside the fiction are going to operate. We suggest that subtle differences in that relationship [and we are not talking about surface qualities of how friendly you are] deeply affect what is learned, how well it is learned and how clearly everyone recognises what has changed in their understanding.

Who are *you*?

One shift of social role is familiar to most role-play leaders. The tutor or teacher can see herself as a 'facilitator'. This appears to reduce the omnipotence of the leader. She is not expected to behave as someone having the answers ready to pass on to a class. She creates opportunities for the class to find the answers themselves. She will usually give the group some kind of limited procedural choice and assist in pacing the experience.

A classic example we have already discussed is AiM's role-play session with hospital ward-managers. The leader behaves very much as a 'facilitator', inviting questions, encouraging decision-making about procedures and posing problems for the class to solve. The facilitator finally invites the class to reflect on their own behaviour and record what they have learnt from the session. Thus s/he does not deliver packaged answers, but, as it were, hides them in the material to be examined. There is an important sense, therefore, in which s/he is indeed well-informed or otherwise she would not know what to hide! What she does not know, and this is crucial, is *how* the answers are going to emerge for *this* particular group. This is how the role-play brings about an *ownership* of knowledge, because that knowledge has grown contextually in two senses. The learners are presented with a sharp, 'live', contextual focus about which they can gain new understanding and they are also active within their own learning context, gaining in self-knowledge about how they set about problem-solving with others.

In the recent past attempts have been made by leaders to be even more self-effacing. Stark examples come to mind of T-Groups in the 1960s in which leaders sit outside a circle of people, simply observing their attempt at group understanding. From the same period we have drama teachers' enthusiasm for spontaneous group creativity insulated from any kind of teacher intervention. Thus the leader can modify the traditional teacher/tutor social role by either elevating it to the level of 'facilitator' or taking it to the extreme of apparent abandonment of responsibility. It is the former, of course, that we recommend.

Who are your students?

If the leader can adjust his social role to affect the tutor/student relationship, that relationship can also become adjusted because the students' cultural role has changed. Some role-plays endow their participants with the cultural role of '**people being tested**' – they know their behaviour is to be inspected. Such an example we have already discussed in the Northern Gas managers' course in which their strengths and weaknesses were exposed by the role-play task analogous with their own situation – but the work was set up in a sufficiently supportive atmosphere that they could make mistakes with impunity – not as in real life. Nevertheless, the sense of 'being tested' was very strong and their high degree motivation and self spectatorship enabled them to test themselves. Another example we have come across is of the Associated Board of Music conducting a simulated instrumental examination in which the performers of all ages and skills agreed to behave as if they were to be 'examination candidates' so that they could be 'examined' by applicants for membership of Associated Board's panel of examiners. It wasn't a 'real' examination, but everyone had to behave as if it were – and on this basis they were selected or rejected. In such simulations 'self-spectatorship', the central feature of role-play, is inevitably to the fore. The facilitator does not have to work to establish it.

The recent history of one's class [in schools it can be as recent as as what happened in the previous lesson!] and the nature of the theme being examined will also determine the extent to which the facilitator needs to work at promoting self-spectatorship. In a role-play session on the theme of 'bullying', those who are already victims are more readily going to function as 'self-spectators' than those in the class for whom the issue is out of their experience. The leader of a session on how ex-psychiatric patients can re-establish themselves in the community, will not have to plan for self-spectatorship if the class is made up of ex-patients. Thus where the participants see themselves as vulnerable **victims** in the particular context being treated as a subject for role-play, 'self-spectatorship' emerges automatically, unless of course their suffering has caused them to set up a barrier against facing their own behaviour. In which case we have to accept the notion of 'negative' self-spectatorship.

Mostly, self-spectatorship has to be planned for – especially so in those who see themselves as having sufficient expertise in the subject-matter. You may be faced with a group of people who do not really see the need for their attending a course or, more constructively, your group may have been selected for their knowledge with a view to finding a way of disseminating it. We could label such classes, '**know-alls**' and '**true experts**', respectively. Examples could be taken from our earlier work – for instance, you could find yourself with a group of apprentice gas-fitters who had the 'know-all' attitude or a group of experienced gas-fitters ['true experts'] who needed to plan a course for their trainees. It is unlikely in either case that 'self-spectatorship' will be in evidence, for neither group will see the need to observe themselves closely. Whatever you plan to do with the groups, you will have to acknowledge how they see themselves, and take 'who they are' as your starting point. In both cases you are going to be respectful of their knowledge and experience, even though you recognise the apprentices' claim as spurious. Another example we quoted earlier referred to a conference on 'bullying in schools' held in Londonderry for nine-year olds who had been chosen to represent each city school. Now, in this instance, the pupils can legitimately see themselves as 'experts' [after all, they are representing their school on the subject], so that when you set up any role-play you will have to take into account that they may well have stereotypic preconceptions and be disinclined to 'see themselves' in the role-play. Again, you must not be tempted to demonstrate how little they really know, but make their 'expertise' your starting point. Our concern is always to 'protect' into the fiction.

Much published advice on how to set up role-play defines the *role* but does not take into account 'who' your class might be at a *real* level, that is, what cultural role in addition to the chosen fictional role they are likely to adopt in relating to the role-play. Let us now look at a typical, one might say, traditional, role-play. Working with a youth group, you set the role-play that begins with the following 'script' [to use the word that traditional simulation practitioners use to describe instructions]:

> You are a teenager and need to ask your parents for permission to stay out till midnight on Saturday night.

And your students take up the idea and proceed to 'invent' a scene. Who are they? They are '**people responding to an instruction**' – and we often require our classes to adopt such a cultural role. They may or may not have a burning interest in the topic – you may have chosen it because you know the issue has cropped up recently. Certainly, you could assume that they are familiar with the subject, in which case they could be described as '***well-informed* people responding to an instruction**'. But supposing you had prepared the ground much more flexibly:

> You discuss with the young people what they saw as a major difficulty at home and when they suggested 'getting permission to stay out late' you invited them to provide 'the script' for a scene and then present it. They instruct three players to demonstrate a teenager asking parents for permission to stay out until midnight on Saturday night.

Now has the cultural role of the students changed? Yes, they are now '**co-operators**' and 'inventors', moving into these roles in response to your shift from 'instructor' to 'negotiator'. But there is something one-dimensional about such an exercise. One feels that the challenge on them as 'inventors' is so slight that aspect of their cultural role is barely worth noting. However, if they were required to depict the parents' many, perhaps contradictory, concerns about an offspring staying out late as, say, an abstract sculpture or collage with perhaps 'voice over', it could be said that they have moved into the cultural role of '**makers**' or '**artists**'.

Your class as 'directors'

'Makers' and 'artists' are broad terms for describing how your class may see themselves. Sometimes their role can be much more specific. An obvious example is when they take on the role of 'directors'. Even very young children can, at least incipiently, take on this kind of responsibility – you only have to watch a small group playing. We have an example in A8 (pp.7-8) when, in setting up six K's to represent an accident sequence, you give your class a chance to suggest 'what kinds of answers they think each K should give when the teacher formally asks each to say what s/he is thinking'.

In D3 (pp.43-44) each group of three gas fitters includes two playing the respective roles of fitter and houseowner with a third taking on the responsibility of 'director' of the scene – and it is the director's influence on 'positive signing' that the audience are invited to comment on.

Similarly, in the work on 'betrayal' with young people, the preparation of the scene in the Garden of Gethsemane (B.9 and 10 pp.20-21) could be in small groups under the eye of an appointed 'director'.

A striking example is in the work of AiM (pp.55-56), in which the hospital manager trainees have the chance to redirect a scene. They have the power to instruct the actor and to stop the scene if they think the actor appears not to understand.

The leader taking a role affects 'who' the class become at a cultural role level

It would be possible to go through all the exercises we have illustrated so far and note whether the participants through their cultural roles are of 'people being tested', 'victims', 'know-alls', 'experts', 'responders', 'co-operators', 'artists' or 'makers'. But what is the position of the participants in all those exercises we have discussed in which the leader has taken on a role within the fiction, teacher-in-role, as it is often called? Here again the answer depends on the extent to which the teacher's function in taking a role is still that of 'facilitator', for sometimes the presentation of such a role places the leader nearer to 'performer' – and the students become **'audience'** to the performance. An example of such a disempowering role would be:

Supposing you are using role to open up the various strands of Emile Bronte's *Wuthering Heights*, a text which your class have read. You decide that an interesting 'way in' to themes of the book would be to consider the strange events occurring in its pages through the eyes of other people living in the neighbourhood.

> So, addressing your class as 'members of the congregation' and introducing yourself as an emissary of the Archbishop with the responsibility for investigating reports of some unholy events occurring in recent months in the midst of this community, you go on with *'This is a close community... and we know that such a community has eyes and ears... we are therefore aware that some persons present must have been failing to disclose to the church... acts which can only be described as sacrilegious... we are authorised by the highest church authority to set up a court of enquiry to investigate... the truth of what has happened here ... no stone, however, innocent looking will be left unturned... and so on... and so on...'*

And no doubt you have done this with proper wrathful authority and conviction! – and your audience will be spellbound! But, of course, the drama is *yours*. Your class have become your 'target' and their cultural role has become that of a mesmerised audience. But you intended that they should adopt the cultural role of 'fellow makers', you and they together making a drama. There are a number of things you could have done. For instance, if, in the preliminary work, you put forward the idea of doing a drama leading to an ecclesiastical enquiry. If they go along with this you could ask them for a good starting idea and if it emerges that they need someone to do the 'emissary' bit, you could ask *'How do you see this person?... is there something I could wear or carry?... how submissive do you want the community to be at this stage?... shall we try it?...'* and picking up the cross or putting on something to represent a stole you begin *'...we have called this community... —— [do I address you as a community or as a congregation...?]—— to this church tonight... to raise a very serious matter, one of concern to the Archbishop himself... and so on... – [now do I ground you down into silence or give you an opening to make comments?]... and so on'*

What you hope now is that your class will begin to feel they are moulding the shape and content of the drama. What they see is you functioning both as negotiating leader and as the character they asked for – they 'read' *both* roles simultaneously. And it may be, on their advice, that you start the scene again in order to insert a new idea, especially if it allows for an early interruption by 'a member of the community', for *their* ownership becomes demonstrated by their contributing in role. Of course a silent community does not *necessarily* mean that your class are failing to own the material. If they have already had the chance to decide that they, as a community, can actually protect themselves from the church authorities by remaining stubbornly silent, then they will enjoy the sense of power this gives them over teacher's role. There is a huge difference between a 'congregation' silent because they are beguiled by teacher's performance or simply at a loss to know how to find a niche for themselves and a 'congregation' *productively* silent because that is the only way of building a wall of resistance. They are now **'fellow-makers'** of the fiction, co-operating with the leader.

You should not conclude from this that in order to share the responsibility, you and your class should always pre-negotiate. For example, if you are in role as a 'witch', saying *'C..o..m..e..i..n...!'* to your class of young children as you open an imaginary door and smile broadly, you want your class to 'read' this as a game and to work hard [and we mean work hard] at refusing to enter. You want them to see you, their teacher, enjoying pretending to set a trap for them while they also see the 'witch' trying to trap them. So your apparently overpowering role is, paradoxically, empowering. You may or may not have prepared your class for the game. You may have begun by saying, '*I think I know how to trick you... just watch!...*' – and you open your door... It may well be that this is your introduction to a very serious topic, knowing that you are really warning them about going off with strangers and that a later step in the role-play is going to be '*What's your name, little girl... Do you like sweets?...*'. So who are they in this kind of role-play? – they *must* be '**winners**'!

Much advice about the use of role-play in therapy deals with the problems to which the role-players are **victims**. It sometimes pays off to set up circumstances unrelated to their particular problem just to let them, for once, have the experience of being **winners**.

A much less spectacular kind of cultural role can be in evidence when you act as 'chairperson' of a meeting which the class attend. They find themselves in role as people who need or demand or are required to attend such a meeting. 'Need' or 'demand' or 'required' appear to be pretty motivating impulses, but the true underlying cultural role is often one of **passive responders**. They are often endowed with some 'opinion' which they are expected to voice at the meeting. In practice they may only have an academic interest in the issue, leaving the leader disappointed in the result. This very common use of 'teacher-in-role' can be labelled 'Swimming Pool' drama, for classically it follows the pattern of chairing a civic meeting at which citizens are invited to say whether extra funds should be allocated for modernisation of swimming pool, sports area, old people's home or library and the sense of drama dies! But there are more stimulating usages of chairmanship.

Let us look at the examples we ourselves have listed, examples in which you lead a 'meeting' of the class as a way of endowing or reinforcing your group's fictional role. In C4 (p.27) we had the leader-in-role as an 'architect' seeking advice from 'doctors' about what they needed to have in their new health clinic. In C9 (p.35-36) the leader, now in role as director of a TV medical series, is addressing 'medical experts', again seeking their advice, this time on what should be included in 'voice overs' about routine medical practice. Both of these examples take the form of a 'meeting' [formal or informal as felt appropriate], but the cultural role of the participants corresponds with the required fictional role – that of **informed advisers**, for they, at both role levels, are seen to have a vested interest in the topic – because they are trainee doctors who one day hope to be experts. Thus there is a problem to be solved and the format of a 'meeting' is used as an authentic medium as it allows the participants to draw on what knowledge they have of an issue they are already committed to and in a style they are familiar with – talk and discussion.

Much more subtle and sophisticated is the example E1 (p.49) in which the leader is certainly addressing a meeting, not in order to endow the Northern-Gas managers with their role, for they are virtually going to 'be themselves', but, rather, to paint an elaborate picture of a fictitious country called Gongua, to outline a project and to establish a whole style of communication appropriate at ambassadorial level. The participants are already highly charged to assess the nature of the task ahead of them.

Given that the 'meeting' can become a platform for the class to express an interest they already hold, then the format of a meeting, with its implied rules of procedure may be useful and protective. The drawback, as we have seen, is that the explicit higher status of the chairperson makes it difficult to help the class feel they are *empowered* by such a format.

Mantle of the Expert – changes both who you are and who your class are

In the work with Northern Gas managers, the group were in role as experts hired to give advice about development of a fictitious third world country and it was their ability to work as a team that was being tested. The structure of this example was that of operating a fictitious context analogous to their normal work – and calling on their expertise as team problem-solvers. In such an exercise their expertise is a 'given' to be examined. It is *not* what we mean by 'Mantle of the Expert'.

'Mantle of the Expert', an approach to education developed over many years by one of the co-authors of this book, Dorothy Heathcote[1], is a sophisticated concept often requiring an elaborate form of implementation over a relatively long school period – two or three weeks, a term or an academic year. The reason for the length of time is that it can cover a whole curriculum and therefore takes as long as would normally be taken to teach whatever has to be taught. Thus it is not an *exercise* in the sense we have been using in this book so far. It is a process that from the beginning sets out to **build a *cultural* role of responsibility through a *fictional* role of running a fictitious enterprise**. So to the question, who are you teaching? The detailed answer is 'a class who have a commitment to carry out tasks worthy of scrutiny'. And what is your social role? Certainly not an instructor, and the label 'negotiator' is inadequate. Your role becomes that of **colleague** to your fellow contributors to the enterprise (your class). This is your *social* role as well as your *fictional* one. You will work at removing your traditional image of being in charge of your students and what they learn. You will not be Mr. Smith, our teacher, but Mr. Smith, our colleague – at least during 'Mantle of the Expert' time – and outside that time your other voice will be that of helper/planner who with your class plans for further tasks. This requires a deep shift in the normal educational practice. Those of you who think that using straightforward role-play is adventurous may well see 'Mantle of the Expert' as foolhardy. It revolutionises our concepts of teaching and learning and dignifies respect for knowledge as paramount.

We can only give a glimpse in this publication of its complexities. We shall attempt to lay bare its principles by giving some details of a plan to teach a Science Curriculum in a Nottingham Primary School.[2] The required curriculum topic for the year's Science was **Air and Wind**. The idea was to make this Science target the central aspect of the Mantle of the Expert project, bringing in (inevitably) other subjects of the curriculum related to humanities, arts, maths and English. For the work to start the teacher has to decide what *enterprise* will most likely fulfil the curriculum matter to be covered, in this case, 'movement of air' and then what choice of fictitious *client* would become the central means of opening up extensive and intensive work on the subject.

You will see there is a time sequence here. Whereas you would have to decide from the very beginning on both the enterprise and the principal client, from your class' point of view, they will experience a series of steps, perhaps lasting but ten minutes at a time, introducing the novel idea that they and you together could run a firm as colleagues, involving your being 'consultants' in this area of science whom '**others**' seek advice from. Outside those brief spells, school life will have its 'normal' teacher/pupil, subject-learning appearance, but as those 'ten minutes' grow longer and closer together, reaching the point when you feel it is right to introduce tasks related to *the* client, the 'normal' school life will recede and 'colleagueness' will sometimes take over. And it will demand hard work which your class may well be glad to have respite from when 'normality' resumes again. But, of course, 'normality' can never be the same again for 'colleagueness', once shared, can never be entirely lost.

The introductory tasks

So you might begin with your Grade 5/6 class with something like: '*Do you think we could turn our science into a drama?... could we become a firm of specialists... consultants... who get paid because we know more than others about wind and air?... and we give them advice...? Shall we have a go?... When I give out these envelopes, could they be the firm's envelopes?... and we're in the middle of doing our usual work... working for this firm...* and in the envelopes you have placed requests for information – from various clients – relating to air and wind {each group has a different task}. They have to be tasks the answers to which you know the class already know or can arrive at e.g. a letter from a student abroad about to study in England, who wants to know what he could expect would be a typical classroom temperature, as he has heard it is very cold in England in winter. And while they are working, so are you [but not sitting at 'teacher's desk'!], with your envelope, asking, say, about the advisability of growing trees on a motor-way grass verge. You may 'think aloud' as you do yours, perhaps at one point asking your colleagues whether they can think of any more pollution problems – in addition to petrol fumes, that is – that are going to affect young trees. You might encourage other envelopes to become 'public' problems – and you can then demonstrate how you, in this kind of drama, are not better informed than they.

At a time 'outside' the drama you might raise the question of what the firm's name and letter heading are going to be. At another time you might invite them to consider how we could make our classroom look more like the firm's office. Reposition the furniture? You encourage them to 'sign' their working surface, perhaps with a 'consultant's name label' or a telephone [drawn] or a computer terminal [drawn] or even a coffee mug [drawn]. You encourage them to individualise their office desks – as you do your firm's desk.

After one or two ten-minute stabs at dealing with envelope tasks, these sessions can become extended – as more time is needed to complete the tasks, until you can reach the point of, [outside the drama] checking that '...what we do... d'you think it seems like what consultants do?...'

When the fiction is accepted you are then ready next time with your invitation from the Garden Festival [When this work was actually done, the idea of the Cardiff Garden Festival 1994 was harnessed. We'll keep referring to Cardiff here, but obviously you will adapt to whatever contexts have contemporary appeal].

You'll have to judge that your class are sufficiently intrigued with the idea that they are a long-established firm to be ready to taken on the major task, for which this 'invisible' character of a key client has to be created. The evidence of such a client arrives through a letter, which you, of course, have written, but you are going to present it as if 'it has just arrived in the post'. We print below the actual letter that was used in the Nottingham primary school:

The National Garden Festival
Administrative Site
Cardiff   24 March, 1991

To: Air Sol
Newcastle

Dear Consultants

I am writing to you to enquire whether you would be able to assist the Committee of the national Garden Festival 1994 on a matter of some urgency.

We had intended to create a very special environment for our visitors to explore, which will help everyone entering it to realise how important the air and atmosphere is to all living things.

We understand that your organisation, AIR SOL CONSULTANTS, are particularly concerned with matters of atmosphere and weather, together with the effects of wind on nature. I am delegated to write to you to ask if you would be willing to advise us on the construction of a 'weather and atmosphere pavilion' in which as many aspects of the air all round the earth, together with how wind is formed and affects plants, soils and rocks, including living creatures – humans and animals – could be experienced and understood by those who visit the Festival in 1994.

We are especially concerned that this 'invisible' matter, air, would be valued by everyone in Cardiff who comes to the Festival. I assure you that we will build whatever you design to your own specifications and funds have been set aside to enable the pavilion to be a high standard regarding its design and construction, together with its contents.

We should also like your ideas on written and illustrated materials which people could take away with them after their visit to the pavilion, so that they would have an opportunity to consider further the place of air in our lives. Also if you have any further ideas for the visitors to participate in any *activities* inside the pavilion to assist their understanding we should be very pleased to hear of them. And we would build what is necessary for those activities. We want people to *participate*, not just to stare at things, if possible. Air is particularly difficult to explain as it is always invisible. However, we are sure you can help us.

If you feel you are able to spare the time and effort it will entail, I, or a member of my Committee will be pleased to come and visit whenever it's convenient for you to discuss the matter.

In the meantime,

I remain

Owen Evans
National Garden Festival, Cardiff

P.S. I quite forgot that, if possible, we should like to invite representatives from those countries where exceptional weather and wind patterns may occur, typhoons, tornadoes, possibly from the Gulf area and the Chernobyl situation, Arctic and Antarctica etc. This will mean that we should include information about these areas to compliment appearances of guests.

The invisible character has a voice, a position, a request, a vision, and an 'air and wind' vocabulary, all of which features are going to be filtered through *your* voice of 'the colleague who has picked up and hurriedly glanced at this morning's late post'. Glanced at but not read. For you are going to *discover* what is in it as you read it aloud [and waving it around as you read it – they have to 'see' the invisible character] to your fellow consultants. Your reading is not going to be straightforward. It will be broken up with your comments – innocuous comments that work to reinforce the credibility of the writer and the status of your colleagues as experts. The whole impression is that you can't wait to share this with them because it seems so important... *'sorry to interrupt what you're doing... but this seems a bit big... I'll photocopy it for everyone for your own files of course... but I thought you'd want the gist...'* And, of course, it's *not* 'the gist', for you must not interpret or summarise – that would keep the power in *your* hands. Your tone is one of wonder – and you can't wait to hear what they have to say about it. You may not get through all of it in one go [literacy hour may be over!!}, but there is nothing to stop you, even 'out of the drama time', bubbling over about *'what it's going to mean for us'*.

You are capturing their interest while inviting them to be in charge of interpreting and replying to that letter. There are two critical hurdles ahead of you. One is to get their agreement to go ahead with the project: *'Do you believe this is a good way of us getting to the Science we need to know about Air and Wind... are you prepared to have a bash and see where it takes us...?'* Only if they are prepared to accept it can the work be done this way. The other hurdle is going to come later when they have formulated and recorded some of their suggestions for creating a pavilion. *'Are we ready, d'you think' to invite Mr. Evans... to show him what we've got so far...?'* For central to this Mantle of the Expert approach to education is that the class should be required to explain what they know to someone else – and the timing has to be right; too soon and they will lose confidence in what they know.

You are no doubt going to be 'Mr Evans', unless you can persuade another member of staff, a parent or a student-teacher to take it on. Whichever way you do it, your *class* must have some say in 'building' him – his outward signals – what he is carrying, how formal/ informal in his style, arriving by car? train etc.. Further than this you may get your class to endow him with a temperament... *'Do you want him to be a chap who doesn't miss a trick... who's done his homework... or a guy who couldn't care less... who's going to have to be taught...?'* This appears to be an important choice for your class to make, but in practice it's the same question in the sense that *both* require curriculum rigour. You may press even further with *'Do you want a guy who likes what you are doing or someone you've got to win over...?'*, a tempting challenge for those Year 5/6 children who are beginning to enjoy confidence in their work and in their 'public' voice.

Thus, whatever style they choose, they are going to have their work examined. The cultural change from what is normally thought of schooling in which a teacher looks at pupils' work is colossal. And if you have timed it right, the educational rewards will be considerable – *and* the current educational policies for science and language will have been met.

Conclusion

In setting up role-play we rush to decide what fictional role our groups should play. We hope this chapter has persuaded you that perhaps the equally important decision is what social role you should adopt and what cultural role your class should be endowed with.

References

1 For a full account see *Drama for learning: Dorothy Heathcote's Mantle of the Expert approach to Education* by Dorothy Heathcote and Gavin Bolton (1995) Heinemann, New Jersey.

2. Further details of this work may be obtained on videos entitled 'making Drama Work' by Dorothy Heathcote and Ian Draper, Audio Visual Centre, University of Newcastle upon Tyne. See particularly tape 12 Drama – Entering the Curriculum (Science Programme).

CHAPTER 6

HOW DO WE TACKLE RACISM?

A teacher who was a victim of a severe racist attack, in reporting her appalling experience to a teacher's conference, Easter 1999, expressed her conviction that a change of attitude in society could only occur if a programme of re-education was to be introduced in schools with four year olds. We instinctively acknowledged the rightness of this without having any ready answers as to how one might set about it. Indeed, what exactly is the *it* we are talking about in respect of such young children? For a young child who witnessed the attack on the teacher or a child brought up in an oppressed ethnic minority or in the household of the oppressor, 'racism' will have a personal meaning even if that particular word is not yet absorbed into the child's vocabulary; but for those who have no such immediate experience it will either not exist even as a pre-formed concept or, insidiously, it may, through barely attended adult talk and actions be planting itself like a dormant seed, a weed, waiting to become part of a young person's value system.

It is the latter we are concerned with here. Whereas the witness to the attack on the teacher may be helped with therapeutic counselling dealing directly with the 'pain' of racism, there is no way of 'directly' dealing with a concept that does not yet exist. Thus in thinking about the education of what we hope is the majority of youngest children in our schools, we cannot tackle *racism* as such. We can only attempt to foster a value system that inhibits the growth of that 'weed'. We need gradually and persistently to build in a set of values honouring humankind.

We may list what such a set of values may include for the youngest age of schoolchild. Our plan of education should embrace experiences leading to the realisation:

That the world is a big place and many kinds of life exist: people, animals, insects, trees, plants and fish.

That they each have special attributes; that such 'difference' is something to be marvelled at.

That all require secure habitats for survival – but special attributes demand different ways of achieving this.

That people by their actions can help to preserve all this variety of life and so benefit from it.

There may be a range of built-in behaviours that a school context can help children exercise in promoting the above. It seems to us that attainment of the required respectful attitude, an *honouring* of living things, is made up of layers of concern:

a compulsion to observe
a compulsion to understand
a compulsion to accommodate
a compulsion to nurture

But such drives can only be achieved through acquisition of their corresponding conceptualisations. One cannot engage *mindlessly* in having respect for living things. It is as much an intellectual thrust as it is a disposition of goodwill. And this is where schooling comes into it own. If teachers regularly provide opportunity for refining those related concepts in a context of caring, the building in of a respectful value system is possible.

The educating route to such concepts is, of course, through the regular application and refinement of **language**. We can teach the language of observing, understanding, accommodating and nurturing and in so doing we are helping our classes to build meaningful concepts. A community of Eskimos have twelve different words for 'snow'. In hearing these words in context, in modelling them and applying them in context, the young Eskimo acquires the appropriate concepts. But, more than that, s/he acquires a tacit understanding of how important it is to have such a range of meanings. The combined language, concepts and attitude become part of the young child's value system.

Thus, if we are to build in our young children a value system that is to stifle the weed of racism, our school classrooms must provide a *cultural* context in which the language of honouring people can be regularly learned and practised, so that concepts underlying the language usage can develop along with a compulsion to care.

Teaching positive attitudes to others, therefore, should be part of the ongoing ethos of a school, but there may be certain kinds of language exercises, that can give a sharp focus to the subject. This is where dramatic role-play has a place.

Please remember that the exercises offered below will be of little value in isolation; they should be seen as but part of that necessary cultural ethos.

'Wallflowers', – from an old playground singing game [to be introduced to kindergarten but gradually extended to older children]

The Yorkshire singing game went as follows. All in a circle sing:

> **Wallflowers, wallflowers**
> **Growing up so high**
> **We're all pretty people**
> **And we've all got to die...**
> **E-x-c-e-p-t-i-n-g...**[*child's name is called*]
> **S/he's 'along of us'**
> **And we look her in the eye**

And that named child goes into the middle of the circle **to be honoured** by the others, who chorally announce: '*We honour you because...*' – and each child in the circle is allowed one briefly spoken compliment: '*I like your hair ribbon*'...'*I like your watch...*'

This introduction to 'honouring' is but a crude first step towards what could become a regular classroom practice, taking on quite elaborate forms, dispensing with the need for the song. The ritualistic form provides a pattern for groupness, for taking turns, for giving each individual a 'big moment' of attention and recognition, for noticing, for noticing what others notice, for selecting brief, supportive words. You can make up your own words for the song, if this Yorkshire one is not to your taste. You will be alert to any need to protect the one 'in the middle' and others may at first need help with 'finding a compliment'. The important thing is that they begin to 'get the *idea*' that there are things about people that can be noticed and voiced. A whole programme of language has begun!

Our first step focused on what someone was wearing. You might smoothly move to other aspects of appearance, colour of hair, height, colour of skin etc. before going on to personality traits, such as 'quiet', 'friendly', 'smiling', 'knows the alphabet', 'can run fast'... each of these *must* ritually be preceded with '*I like...*' Your particular children may find these difficult to think of on the spur of the moment, so you may need to prepare the ground: '*When we play our game... I wonder what kind of thing we will like about people... what kind of thing we will notice about so and so...?*'.

This is a very personal game, but it can also prepare the ground for a much wider consideration. The child in the centre can *represent* something or someone else, merely carrying a sign to say who or what s/he is – endangered creatures or animals that humans rely on or anything from the natural world. It is much more demanding now to select a whole range of attributes and to find the relevant vocabulary.

As your class (now older than the four year olds we began with) become practised in the game, the 'wallflower' (or whatever you have made up) chant can be cast on one side *while retaining the notion* of 'honouring time' and keeping some sense of ritualistic form. For instance, whoever has cropped up in any aspect of the curriculum as an important figure – from science, history, the arts, the news – can be given a central place. '*Who shall be honoured this week?...* might become a regular classroom feature. And the whole thing can become more complex by your introducing the idea that instead of it being a one-way interaction, it can become a question and answer ritual, with each in the 'circle' posing the question and the one in the middle finding the answers, perhaps justifying his/her right to be so chosen. We have now gone far beyond the surface 'observation' with which this ritual began with the very young, to a search for answers to why some people become the makers and menders of the world, their motives, the cost to their lives, and the sacrifices to themselves and others.

And a sophisticated tension may have crept in of wanting to respect the chosen person, while having some reservations about certain aspects. The ritual now shifts to a mature level of making one's criticisms explicit *within* a framework that never loses a basic respect for another person as a person. When you have reached this point with your classes you will have established a model code of classroom practice that you hope will be reflected in their lives out of school. You have also laid down a procedure for handling all kinds of dramatic role-play. The 'person in the centre of the circle' can now be replaced by all kinds of dramatic depictions – still pictures, tableaux, enactment of situations – all to be interrogated and *honoured*. The original singing game has virtually disappeared altogether but its *spirit* of groupness, of close observation and caring remain.

'O1! Get off the train'[1] **Grade 1.**

If our overall purpose is 'honouring', you may feel inclined, as a reminder to your class of humankind's basic instinct to *reject* rather than honour, to slip in a ritualistic game in which individuals first suffer (fleetingly!) rejection until they *appeal* to the rest of the group for protection. The picture story, *Oi! Get off the train*, is a dream sequence in which a child imagines himself and his favourite soft toy, driving and firing an express steam train through all sorts of weather conditions. Each time they return to the train after playing in the fog, the river or the snow, they are faced with various endangered species (elephant, walrus, marsh bird, tiger and polar bear) who have boarded the train in their absence. Their immediate reaction is '*Oi! Get off the train*', but when the creature explains its circumstances, the other creatures and the boy listen to their appeal – and the new creature joins the community.

Having shown this picture book to your class of young children, you could make up a ritual in which a line of 'intruders' in turn sit on one of the seats of the train (a line of empty chairs except for the front two occupied by the 'boy' and 'his toy'). To the chorus of '*Oi! Get off the train*' they have to respond with a description of why they are endangered – and then they are allowed to stay on the train, joining in the initial rejection of the next one. You and the class could agree on what are the most welcoming words to be repeated each time.

Amy Johnson and the food of the world – Grade 2

For this your class take an advisory and problem-solving role over a long period of time such as a school term. Stimulated by the fiction of a private plane flyer (could be Amy Johnson, as indeed it was when Dorothy Heathcote did this work) intending to fly round the world, the 'drama' begins with her having to make an emergency landing, because of fuel shortage, in someone's back garden. From telling her where she is and asking her where she is going, they discover she has a very limited idea, only having a blank map with but one place named.

They list for her all the 'safe' and 'dangerous' places they know of and then start to advise her on where she should go next in the world, first researching for her as much information as possible relating to people, their kind of life, customs, climate and food. They gradually build her a route map of countries and towns. After 'visiting' each place, the pilot reports back to the class for advice on the next place and particularly becomes interested in reading stories [stories collected in readiness by the children who proceed to read them to her] about the place before going there. Where possible you bring in a local person who originally comes from the 'next' country, who, arriving with photographs, artifacts and costumes is prepared to answer questions – s/he might even prepare an ethnic food dish for all to dip into!

You can either play the role yourself of a pilot (leather gauntlets, goggles and high boots can suggest 'Amy Johnson') or, less satisfactory, you can establish her by 'letter' or 'radio message'. Her 'presence' has to be sufficiently credible and stimulating to launch your class on a lot of work sustained over a period of time.

What is important, of course, is that you are creating a collective understanding among your class that the world is peopled with real beings whose difference from us is hugely interesting and to whom our 'pilot' *must learn to accommodate*. Part of each week may be set aside to prepare the information awaiting her return from the current flight.

Understanding an other's needs – **Key-Stage 1**

Continuing our purpose of helping young children to develop an awareness of other cultures in the world, this work carried out by Dorothy Heathcote in America, also focuses on third world needs and some of the responsibilities that go with giving and receiving.

Dorothy used a 'Mantle of the Expert' approach. She built a dairy farming enterprise with her pupils, her role being that of 'manager'. Each child is responsible for one milch cow, each cow being given a name and a 'stall' with feeding mangers and drinking trough [all indicated with two dimensional labels and paintings – 'leading' ropes' drawn by each name].

Cows are milked, washed, watered, fed and led out to pastures where a bull 'guards' them. Each cow's life history is invented and portrait painted. A vet is called in who announces they are in calve. They prepare the barn for when they are born [scanning shows that they are all female].

One day, an Indian lady with a bundle (baby) comes and asks whether she could have a calf to take back to India so that her baby could have good milk. She explains how cows are sacred and the calf will be cared for. She carries a newspaper headline:

Farmers agree to each send a calf to India and Africa to help bring milk to village children

And this is why she has come to see them. What to do? Which calf? How to choose? How to transport? Conditions on arrival? How will people learn to look after?

The class interrogate lady, who brings more information – pictures of her village, her family, her home, the weather.

Class make a guidebook explaining every detail of cow management. An official comes who will arrange to ship the calf when it is old enough. Children interrogate regarding conditions of the aircraft.

Forms of giving and receiving are signed.

But how to choose which one!? paintings are made of each calf. Vet examines each calf. Colours are considered with lady – how do people in India value colour?

Select by drawing lots? 'musical calves' [instead of chairs!] blind-fold vet and have calves in line? Let baby choose? – your class will decide.

Final handing over ceremony.

This Mantle of the Expert role experience invited young children to consider responsibilities towards our world and the 'third world[2]'. Let us now take an example, for older children, of how it is not always easy to take on responsibility for a needy person. Refugees fleeing from Kosovo come to mind.

'The Starveling'[3] Key-Stage 2/3

Written in sophisticated language, this is a country story about a group of isolated villagers' attitudes to looking after an abandoned kitten. They all, including the kitten's fellow creatures such as the mother cat and the fox, have good reasons for not taking it in. The creatures' response is instinctive and a matter of survival; the adults' is 'sensible' and soundly practical in its anticipation of even more problems if they were to take it in, their commonsense suitably over-laid with a proper degree of pity and guilt. The neighbours concur in their regretted rejection and are united in their condemnation of the 'didicais' gypsy family whose sudden departure caused the kitten to be left behind.

If we were to re-read the above summary and replace 'kitten' with 'refugee', we would understand that '...*they all had good reasons for not taking him in...*' – that their intentions were good and that they knew who to blame. We suggest that your class can, having read the story, translate it into dramatic episodes, using parallel attitudes, but now faced with a *refugee* 'at the door'. Returning to the story, how-ever...

One character, has reasons that are neither sensible nor practical. If there is pity and guilt, such feelings are long suppressed by her own tragic experience many years before. That occurrence moulded a bitterness that the kitten at the end of the story begins to crack... 'She [Miss Coker] stooped and with an abrupt movement passed her hand over its body. It was the first time in fifteen years that she had allowed herself to fondle a living creature, animal or human, lest this should be taken from her...'.

A challenge to your class is to understand the rationalisations of the neighbours in a refugee context and to enter Miss Coker's history sufficiently to find the equivalent, in a refugee context, of her abrupt bending down to touch so that she in turn is 'touched'.

In small groups, they could script, rehearse and show separate moments of their new story.

John Brown, Rose and the Midnight Cat[4], Key-stage 1/2

Rose lived with her dog, John Brown. 'We are all right, John Brown', said Rose. 'Just the two of us, you and me'. But she reckoned without the mysterious midnight cat, and it was John Brown who realised that things were going to change.

These are the opening lines of a child's picture book, perhaps aimed at 4-6 year olds, but as Pam Baddeley and Chris Eddershaw point out in their brilliant analysis (including research on children's reactions to *John Brown, Rose and the Midnight Cat*) of how children read pictures,[5] older children will have greater insight into possible meanings. For the best role-play work you will need to have a copy of the book available for your class to study, although there is a video which may be a useful alternative.[6]

It is essentially a story about relating with outsiders. A stray cat is welcomed by the widow, Rose, threatening the cosy, mutual affection long-shared with her dog, John Brown, who does all he can to undermine Rose's new plan, but retreats into sulky acquiescence – well, for now! – while Rose beams contentedly and the Midnight Cat purrs.

Whatever role-play is set up must put you in a position where you have the 'authority' to ask questions about what is going on in that household and where your class can search for answers that go beyond 'what's going on' to understanding *why* and to *anticipating* new outcomes. You should avoid requiring your class to 'act out the story' – their attempt at dramatisation would merely diminish the artistry of the combined pictures and narrative of the publication.

Drama enthusiasts sometimes overrate their art by assuming that somehow drama can replicate, and thereby enhance, the original medium. It is our view that any dramatisation should throw light on the story without copying it.

That sufficient degree of authority would be available to you if you could therefore take the role of 'a social worker', building up a 'case-study' of the goings on at Rose's cottage, and your class could be people who have studied the 'relevant documents' – that is, the book. You can invite your class in groups of six to show *one moment* in the story's events. Three children can carry labels showing which of the three characters they are and, standing behind each, three 'speakers of their thoughts', one to each character. Each group of six will show their selected moment in turn with you examining each picture, saying what you observe, and asking questions about motives and feelings of each character – writing down what they explain. Then follows a discussion on what should happen now in that household. How can the uneasy, final compromise be maintained to assist the three to develop their future lives? You may invite the class to invent new tricks on the Midnight Cat that John Brown might get up to behind Rose's back, if something isn't done.

Their answers may stay with practical solutions at first, but you have to find a way of steering them towards **what will the Midnight Cat and John Brown have to learn in order to respect each other?** And what will Rose have to understand about John Brown's feelings? We are near here to the 'pain' of racism, where there is destruction rather than accommodation and where deepest feelings tend to be dealt with by pretending they are not there.

Children aged six to eleven may find these concepts difficult to grasp, and perhaps impossible to articulate. However, the illustrations in the picture book can often allow children to 'sense' these things without 'knowing' them. In the research Pam Baddeley and Chris Eddershaw conducted with children aged 4-11, even a four year old, when asked whether Rose should have insisted on John Brown letting in the Midnight Cat answered

'*No, she was wrong because he did not like the cat*[7]',

demonstrating an acceptance that some don't like others and, further, an understanding that this is something in itself that has to be respected. Interestingly, an 11 year old did not go as far as acknowledging this latter point. Her answer was

> *'Rose could have said something nice and reassuring to John Brown to make him feel more that he wasn't going to lose his place, he wasn't going to be kicked out because Rose wanted a cat.'*[8]

No concern here for John Brown's basic *dislike* of cats, just a 'smoothing over'.

When we invite children to comment on a character's feelings in a story, we must expect their answers to relate to those characters' reactions to the new event and in this instance, you can expect from your class suggestions that 'John Brown was worried at being pushed out' or 'The Midnight Cat wanted to come into the warm' or 'John Brown was jealous'. It is most unlikely that you will hear your class probe *beyond* the context of the new event for their answers. **And yet this is where feelings relating to racism lie**: John Brown hates cats **for that is how life is!** His attitude goes beyond the particular context.

One possible way of reaching this level of understanding, from as early an age as possible, is continually to give one's class some insight into the idea of *levels* of answers, an understanding that any action can be explained in more than one way and that they can use dramatic presentations to practise changing the level.

It is worth examining these 'levels of motivation' and their implication for racism in some detail:

Levels of Explanation

If we see someone perform a simple, everyday action, say, 'picking up litter', it may be self-explanatory – the meaning of the action lies in the action itself – the picking up of litter. But if we wanted to press for another dimension of meaning we could ask him *why* he was picking it up – and now his explanation lies within the category of **Motivation** and his answer might be: *'Because I am tidying it* *away'*. He has given us an explanation which identifies his objective, but really does not tell us very much. We might press further and seek how much **Investment** his motivation carries. Moving to this level he might offer all sorts of answers (that go beyond the particularity of the immediate action to some awareness of such matters as taste, responsibility, and consequences etc): *'I can't bear to see a place untidy'*; *'I think everyone should do their bit.'*; *'What a mess this place will look if we didn't tidy up.'* Such answers give both psychological and social dimensions to his motivation.

But there are deeper explanations for his actions. He is part of a *cultural* order that underpins all his behaviour. Consciously or not he *models* all his actions on an other's standards. The 'other' may be as overarching as 'what we do in the Western world' to as narrow as 'my mother used to say...' Such 'models' need not necessarily be of the past – a family moving from a Council to a 'Yuppie' estate may urgently seek new models. Thus our litter-gatherer's deeper explanations, if really pressed, may veer towards: *'We were brought up to be tidy'* or *'The front of our house matches our neighbours for tidiness'.'*

We have, then, four levels of explanation:

The Action – self-explanatory
The Motivation – the 'immediate' explanation relating to the particular objective
The Investment – a 'generalising' explanation, relating to all actions of this kind.
The Cultural Model – an authorisation

But there is another. Our action may still be insufficiently explained by any of the above. It may be embedded in our value or belief system. At this level our man may answer: *'Tidiness is next to cleanliness and godliness'* or *'All matter is part of nature's recycling which we must foster'*. **This is how life is**. This is the level of John Brown's hatred of cats [and this is the level of Miss Coke's sterile reaction to others, in *The Starveling*, above] – he has no choice in the matter; it is an unalterable definition of life. And this, as we have said, is the impenetrable level at which racism may operate. If we expect someone who is already racist to change his attitude, we may be asking him to change what can't be changed, his very definition of life. This is why the injured victim who addressed the teacher's conference advised that education in anti-racism must start with four year-olds – before racism becomes embedded at this deepest level of values.

We have, then, *five* levels of explanation: 1. The Action; 2. The Motivation; 3; The Investment; 4; The Cultural Model; 5. This is how life is.

Let us look at a racist action:

1. **Action** – A girl yells at another girl, '*Get back to your own country you black bastard!*'

Asked why she did this might require the following kinds of explanations:

2. **Motivation**: '*She sat where I was going to sit on the 'bus*'

3. **Investment**: '*She's lucky I didn't beat her up*'; or '*She's trying to pinch my best friend from me*', or '*I'm not going to let her get away with anything.*'

4. **Cultural Model** (if really pressed): '*Everyone says they're black bastards*'; or '*My Dad says they should be locked up.*', or '*They're taking our jobs – everyone knows that*'.

5. **This is how life is**: '*England is for the English – as long as they're white*'. or '*Black's unlucky.*'; or '*You can't trust coloured people*'.

A mistake that can easily be made in attempting to tackle a problem arising from a racist incident is to treat the Action and Motivation levels of behaviour, as though there is nothing deeper. 'Why did you do that?' asks an authority figure of a racist – and the answers stay at the Action and Motivation level, a shrug of the shoulders or a '*He started it*'. And so the focus remains on who started what, which has nothing to do with the deeper reasons. A complementary mistake is to acknowledge that there are indeed deeper levels than action and motivation but that they are fixed in cement. This, as we have suggested, may be true for level 5, but level 4, the 'cultural model' may be open to change. It is sometimes the case that in breaking away from immediate cultural models that an adolescent can grow up. An obvious example is that of an adolescent whose father was an alcoholic, a model to be resisted. Helping racist young people to identify what answers they could give – at least to themselves – at different levels, might be the first step towards a re-education.

But, going back to John Brown, we suggest that an education that sets out to make children aware that there *are* such levels in the way others' actions can be explained, is also a process of gradually building the *capacity* to examine their own actions at all levels, a capacity to recognise flaws. Such an awareness training provides a *preventative* education against racism – or against any other 'weed' waiting to be nurtured. It may be impossible for young children to recognise their own value system dictating 'This is how life is', but they *can* learn to look for such a deep level of explanation of behaviour in the characters within a fiction, in this case of *John Brown, Rose and the Midnight Cat*.

In the exercise suggested above (p.138), your class were to select still moments from the story and each character was to have a partner, a 'speaker of their thoughts' standing behind, responsible for explaining their actions. Now if you can introduce your children (adapting the labelling of the categories to their age group) to these 5 levels, the questions from the audience to each performing group and the subsequent answers from the three spokespersons may become more subtle and penetrating as they begin to understand the level shifts. Let us look at the kind of answers you might hope for:

John Brown

1. Action – (from the last picture in the book) '*I am sitting with my back to the other two, sulking.*'

2. Motivation – '*I am feeling pushed out by that creature.*'

3. Investment – '*If I sulk Rose will feel sorry and she'll have to get rid of the Midnight Cat.*'

4. Cultural Model – '*I have learnt that a dog like me should not be expected to suffer such indignity, but I have also learned to please Rose.*'

5. This is how life is: '*Dogs hate cats; I hate cats; I love Rose –
    she's all I've got.*'

And such probing can be done for each of the characters. When the
scenes are over, perhaps another day, you might pose the question,
'What can they do?'; 'How *should* life be!!?? And here you are
introducing the notion of compromise – and how hurtful is the
compromise when you have to compromise at Level 5, the defining
layer of our lives.

This is the question we want everyone concerned with racism to ask.

References

1 *Oi! get off the train* by John Burningham Jonathan Cape London 1989

2 For an example of how children's literature, aimed at 4-7 years of age, can deal directly with
people whose lives are different we recommend *Sharpa Lives in India* by Jean Harrison (Ed)
[accompanying Teacher's book by Marianne Heathcote Woodbridge] Christian Aid, London
1999

3 *The Starveling* by Nina Warner Hooke Putnam, London 1958

4 *John Brown, Rose and the Midnight Cat* by Jenny Wagner, illustrations by Ron Brooks
Puffin Books, Penguin Books Harmonsdworth. The Children's Book Council of Australia,
Picture Book of the Year Award, 1977.

5 *Not so simple picture books* by Pam Baddeley and Chris Eddershaw, Trentham Books,
Stoke-on-Trent, 1994

6 Video 246 Weston Woods

7 Pam Baddeley and Chris Eddershaw ibid p.68

8 *ibid.* p.69

CHAPTER 7

ROLE-WORK WITH THE POLICE ON RACISM – 'STEREOTYPING'

Throughout this book we have been conscious that our expertise does not necessarily lie within the material we have been using as examples of role work. We are certainly not experienced infant teachers, gas-board apprentices, doctors, nurses, dietitions, designers, factory managers or Shakespearean scholars. And here we are having the gall to address trainers of police officers on the subject of racism, as though we know their job. This is far from the case. All we can do is to suggest that an action-based course where participants take different roles might have some appeal to those responsible for police-training.

The Chief Constable of Northumbria, in a recent address to the Tyne and Wear Racial Equality AGM[1] made the following statement:

> 'Within Northumbria Police, I have introduced a policy called **'Dignity in Action'** which deals with all types of harassment – racial, sexual or bullying. It sets out clearly what behaviours we expect from our employees and what behaviours will not be tolerated. Out commitment is absolute – we enforce it rigorously and will take disciplinary action where necessary.'

Given this stringent policy, one may wonder whether our recommendations will be superfluous. It is possible, however, that Northumberland Police may not be typical either in respect of their visionary approach to racism nor in the number of racial incidents.

When we considered, in the last chapter, how an educational programme with four year olds might tackle racism, we soon realised that one cannot hope to deal with anti-racist attitudes directly: one can only attempt to educate young children into a respect for persons. Likewise, when we consider tackling racism among adults, we would be fantasising if we claimed that some role-play programme could effectively change people's attitudes and behaviour. If I am racist, only some traumatic experience in my own life could eradicate the stance I have built up over the years. No *course* is going to change me – it might indeed serve to *reinforce* my negative attitude to ethnic groups. It might indeed reinforce my *denial* that I am racist.

What a course *may* be able to do is to help the participants appreciate how racism is but part of a broader infectious disease penetrating society – that of **stereotyping**. It may also demonstrate how stereotyping can go very deep in our individual and communal value system – and how, not just our actions, but the *language* we use perpetuates the disease. In other words, a course may help us look differently at how we tend to perceive other people.

How we perceive others is often dictated, not by what there is to see, but by how we have been taught to see. This is especially true of a close-knit community, people who live together or work together. We build our *own* group identity through tacitly agreeing on how we want to see others. Teachers build there own status by the way they refer to their pupils; religious groups build their own image of themselves by the way they perceive those 'not of our faith'; employers are what they are because they have employees [the move towards joint ownership for some implies loss of identity!]. Each of these groups, along with prisoner officers, nurses, ship's crews, office staff, miners, a closed order of nuns and firemen, creates a language code that reinforces who they are and their differences from others outside their 'enclave'.

Now some of these groups are distinctive because they have a *professional* commitment to 'those outside', often thought of as 'the general public'. They are required to be especially good at 'perceiving others'. This is especially true of the police whose job is to serve and protect the public. But they also need protecting from the public. They are often treated with cynicism and suspicion and are sometimes subjected to danger. Perhaps more than any other group they need to bolster each other's identity, a side effect of which can be a tacitly agreed stereotyping of others. It is not that individually they are more sexist, racist, homophobic or ageist than the rest of us, but their own sub-culture can exacerbate such negative biases. Their 'in house' style of vocabulary may be protective, colleague-boosting, economical and even witty, while at the same time unintentionally reducing sections of the public to inferior stereotypes – and, no doubt, inducting new colleagues into following suit!

The police in turn experience what it is like to become the stereotype of members of the public. While working as a writer in residence at various penal institutions, Tom Hadaway[2] was handed a piece of writing by an inmate which compared a prison to a 'hotel of one bedroom apartments' with a 'village shop' and 'local post office'. The metaphor continued:

'Further enquiries,
Nearest police station,
To be '*fitted up*' and recommended' (our italics)

Any training of police officers must take into consideration aspects of entrenched bias and stereotyping from the public which will influence their contact with the community, this, in addition to recognising the possibility of excessive stereotyping in themselves. Can role work help?

Can role work help?

Role work as part [a *small* part!] of training of police officers may:

1. prepare them to face unpredictable behaviour (positive and negative – it isn't all threatening!) from individuals and groups.

2. invite them to recognise and acknowledge their own entrenched views about people.

3. help them to examine their own habits of thought and judgements about others' behaviour and appearance.

Using role as part of training seems particularly appropriate because of the way it brings participants face to face with situations which can be worked through. This has an a immediacy and concreteness not usually present in a theoretical lecture – although that will have its place.

Unless actors are available for the work as instanced in AiM's example on hospital ward management (p.53-56) you will have to use police officers who are members of your class to 'stand in' for the various non-police roles you will require. We use the term 'stand in' deliberately, as it must be made clear from the beginning and continually reinforced that no-one is to expect *acting*. Officers will simply take it in turn to indicate a role, trying to demonstrate an attitude and a language that fit logically from the instructions given before the role-play. Indeed, you will set up the exercises in such a way that interruption from others is normal procedure – so that there cannot be any sense of a play being enacted or a story being told.

Plan for holding a two day course with Police Officers on 'Stereotyping' related to 'Racism'

It may be that the police training course should begin with the idea of every action being underpinned by a deeply ingrained value system. So,

Step 1

Written large on a flip-chart:

Action
Motivation
Investment
Cultural model
This is how life is

You begin with: '*I'm going to do something quite ordinary... and turn it into something extraordinary...*' And you demonstrate picking up a dropped toffee paper and putting it in a waste-paper basket.

You then explain that under every action there can be all sorts of obvious and unobvious meanings. '*Let's get the obvious out of the way...*' And you proceed with asking your class to suggest a label for the action. Whatever they come up with you fill in on the flip-chart. Likewise, a 'Motivation' label.

You then ask if there might be a 'hidden' agenda. Could I have an *investment* in tidying up? – that I can't bear to see anywhere untidy etc. Write down whatever they come up with.

And then introduce the idea of 'authorisation', that I *learnt* to behave in this way from my past upbringing or the pressure of present circumstances – e.g. 'I want to impress others with my orderliness!' – a 'cultural model'.

Finally, invite your class to find a deeper value, something in me that in the disposing of litter is *ineradicable* – e.g. we have a responsibility for the environment and the recycling of waste.

Step 2

Having introduced the process to your class [let us assume it is a class of 16 police officers], now make sure they realise it does not just apply to 'good' deeds:

With a nearly-eaten apple in your fist and a half-sandwich in a plastic bag, explain that the two chairs you have laid out represents the fence of someone's front garden and that you are standing on the pavement in front of it. With a deliberate aim toss your apple core and the rest of your litter over the 'fence' – and ask your class in pairs or fours to write down what should *now* go on the flip-chart [during which exercise you do not retrieve the offending litter, even though it is your instinct to do so! – it must remain there to be stared at until the exercise is over] – assuming the observers can get at a 'truth' behind the action i.e. not necessarily the answers the offender would want to give if s/he were asked!]

Step 3

Having discussed their suggestions, unless any one of them has racist implications, you now ask:

Keeping to your same teams of four, see what you come up with if the offender is white and the owner of the house is black. You discuss their lists and then introduce the idea of it being the other way round – the 'thrower' black.

You will have given some thought to introducing such an obviously explicit racist context so early in the course. There is an argument for delaying this degree of explicitness and allowing it to develop more naturally from the later work on 'stereotyping'. However, this is a relatively short course and you may feel it is right to take the plunge.

Step 4

As your group appear to grasp the process invite them to do the same for a typical racist incident, one that is so common it often gets ignored:

You describe the following incident: On a school bus [using the example similar to the one quoted in our last chapter] a white girl, Sarah, makes a black girl, Janice, give up her seat and go to the back of the bus, by saying '*That's my seat you black bastard!...*' You again discuss their suggestions [again, from their point of view as observers, not the answers Sarah might choose to give] and write one set on the flip-chart, for example:

Action: racist, bullying behaviour and racist, abusive language on bus.
Motivation: she wanted that seat
Investment: she always tries to get the better of 'them'
The Cultural Model: It's what her friends do
This is how life is: it's a matter of *power* and it's *fun* and 'they' should be kept in 'their' place.

Now pose the question of who might want to change the offender's behaviour, on hearing of the incident. They may suggest a head-teacher, the police, social worker or a priest. Follow this with: '*And at what* level *is it conceivable that change could occur?...*' Your class may feel that some person of authority could put a stop to Sarah behaving badly on the bus, but not have any 'deeper' effect.

Demonstrate the *absurdity* of such a reprimand from authority being seen as some serious anti-racist measure. On a large card write boldly whatever they have chosen for This is how life is. In our example it would read:

It's a matter of *power* and it's *fun* and they should be kept in their place

Now invite one of your class to represent a headteacher to whom the incident has been reported. S/he will address you as if you are the offending pupil, ask you for your version and reprimand you. But *you* are sitting or standing there holding the large card in front of your chest like a breastplate – a 'sign' cancelling out your apologetic words.

You will then re-play the scene with another member of the class [try to invite volunteers and select one who you know can cope with the 'impasse' feel the scene is bound to have] in role as a police officer giving Sarah a 'warning' – and getting the same apologetic response. This time your 'mother' [another from your class] is standing beside you – silent.

You re-play the scene and invite members of the class in turn to stand behind the silent parent, speaking aloud her private thoughts.

You may want to allow time here for discussion in groups on whether one's deepest values can ever be changed, especially in connection with racism. You have deliberately focused the exercises leading up to this discussion on 'members of the public' who are racist and examined their hypothetical levels of motivation, but you hope that your own police officers will apply these levels to themselves – and privately examine their own racist, or sexist value system. Private, it is and private it should remain, if you hope to have further cooperation on this course!

Step 5

But now you are going to shift the ground slightly, but significantly. Significantly for police work, that is:

'*Supposing...* [you begin]*... the incident did occur between Sarah, a white girl, and Janice, a black girl... Sarah did make Janice move from her seat, but simply said: 'That's my seat...'. The phrase 'you black bastard' was not said at all, but was* reported *as having been said by Janice...'* Ask your class how this slant could affect Sarah's 'levels of motivation'. Can they think of scenarios about which a totally different interpretation could be made, the only stable feature being that she did say '*That's my seat*' and she did make Janice move?

Ask them to keep their ideas to themselves for the moment, get into teams of four [let's assume there are four teams of four] and work out such a scenario, the two observers drafting out possible 'levels of motivation' for *both* characters. Invite some groups to show their solution, withholding their 'motivation' levels until the scene is over and the audience have had the chance to suggest what might be on their new list.

Thus you have launched your class onto playwriting! They have to *visualise* new possibilities – not easy. ..you may need to help teams as they get stumped.

Their choice' of motivation levels' for Janice may establish that *she* is the one who should have been reprimanded by the headteacher, but life is unfair and it is *Sarah* who has caught the attention of the authorities.

Step 7

You will discuss both girls' motivation levels, of course, but for the purpose of the course you will steer the focus back to Sarah.

Ask your class to select from the range of lists the one that most appeals to them as a clear contrast to the list she was first given. It might read something like:

Action: Sarah says firmly: 'That's my seat'
Motivation: Wanted to sit with her friend; Janice had pushed in
Investment: No tolerance for 'pushy' people, even though she quite likes Janice.
Cultural Model: Her parents taught her to stick up for what's right without hurting others.
This is how life is: She knows that sometimes fighting for 'rights' risks hurting others.

Now you want your class to have the visual image of a 'misreading' by the police. Ask the person you selected before if s/he could now re-play the role of the police officer 'warning' the 'racist offender' – and play it as near as possible to what happened before – the same questions, the same words of warning. **But** this time *you* will be holding up a totally different card against your chest. Should you be questioned about 'racist' language you will deny it but for the rest you will be your apologetic self as you feel some guilt about the way you treated Janice. The 'officer' will take your denial as spurious and press on with his/her warning.

The purpose of the first playing of the scene with Sarah was to bring home to your class how unrealistic it is to assume than any warning or punishment by an authority representative of society can affect someone's values below the most superficial. The second playing had a rather different purpose. You have deliberately set up a 'mis-reading' of an event. You now explain to your class that how they as police officers are expected to perceive people and events will become the basis of the rest of the course.

Part of the skill of 'reading' people and events is to notice detail, but a less obvious part of effective 'reading' is to suspend judgement while waiting for full facts. It is very difficult not to jump to conclusions, to 'fill in' gaps by stereotyping what information one does have. You learn that a witness is a retired schoolmaster, but it turns out he retired last year aged 49 because of ill health. You learn that a witness is a vicar's wife – true, but she is also a financier. And yet in each case you allowed yourself to have a 'picture' in your head. One has to be aware of oneself doing this. But there is a more sinister aspect to 'reading': the danger of bringing one's own value system to bear on what one sees. This is where, without realising it, one can allow one's own racist, sexist, homophobic leanings to bear on one's judgements of a person or situation.

Let us tackle shortage of facts first.

Step 8

Using the 'retired schoolmaster' and 'vicar's wife' as examples ask the class to jot down in their foursomes three similarly sterotypic categories. As honestly as possible tell each other what 'comes to mind' when one reads or hears that category – and then invite them to add a feasible, but distorting feature to each. Show the list to another group, withholding the extra features, asking the other group to add their own extra features – and then compare results. The whole class can share some of the ideas.

Step 8 has provided a little light relief after concentrating on the implications of 'Sarah', but you need to move to more demanding exercises that are going to help officers to see how they may, without realising it, rely on such unintentional, innocent stereotyping in their work.

In preparation for the next steps you should make the following documents:

An 'identikit' picture (male or female) which has any special features noted – not too distinctive in respect of 'economic class' for we later want to place the person in a variety of housing environments.

A written statement. It must appear sufficiently authentic to police work without it being exactly correct, for example:

Station No.————————————————

Crime No.—————————————————

Time of message:————————————————

Date of message————————————————

Duty Officer—————————————————

Witness Account (You can select male or female)

The witness, Mrs. Caroline James, working in the Post Office in Weston High Street reported seeing a man (subject of identikit document) loitering. The time being just prior to closing of the premises. She had noticed this exactly having checked their clock, locked the safe and was in process of approaching the metal outer door shutter to make the premises secure when she noticed a car stopping. Thinking it was a customer bringing late franked mail she waited. Two men approached very fast. Her keys were snatched from her and she was locked in a storeroom at the back of the premises. She thinks the 'loiterer' was still around when the car arrived. She suggested he was 'in on it'.

Police Constable Norman's account

I was on beat, about to report in at Wrekenton Post Office point. All had been as it should be. I went to the back of the premises and noted a small window open and heard calls for help from inside. I summoned assistance and released the post office attendant who gave me the above account.

Duty Officer's note

The witness was brought to this station, comforted and a written statement obtained, prior to being taken home in a police car.

The identikit was prepared by duty artist.

3. Some cards labelled 'witness' with further information written on back. Examples might be:

Witness is known to be of a nervous disposition

Witness owns the shop attached to the Post Office

Premises have recently changed hands

The site is a gathering point for school children who buy lunch time sandwiches and people queueing for fish and chips and kebabs from a nearby cafe which opens at 8p.m.

Witness's ex-husband has a record for petty theft

Witness thought that the men were 'coloured', although she didn't see them properly

4. Some photographs or pictures from magazines of four (one will be for each group) contrasted properties.

Step 9

You ask your class once more to work in their teams of four, giving a copy of the 'Witness' Account', PC Norman's report, and the Duty Officer's note to each officer. You ask them to treat these reports as if they were all written just a few hours ago soon after the woman was discovered – and that they, the 'day shift' team, are to pick up the threads. [You may need to win their agreement to take this on – if they don't the rest of your course is in shreds! Hopefully they have become suffiently intrigued by the previous exercises]. Aware that the course is now about their ability to 'perceive' neutrally, they are invited by you to read the documents without at first consulting each other, and immediately to jot down (doesn't have to be tidy!) the absolute 'facts' and 'absence of facts' and also to note whether there was any part of the documents where they found themselves in danger of jumping to conclusions. Have they already formulated questions that need to be asked of the writers of the reports and the witness? Have they already started to 'put the incident together' in their minds? All these things they now discuss within their groups.

Step 10

You now hand one plain card to each group – with just one item of extra information on, such as:

Witness owns the shop attached to the Post Office

Their team discusses whether this extra information adds anything to the picture they have so far. From the 'evidence' they have, they now plan how they will approach the witness for the purpose of getting further details of the event. As they work on this you will go round reminding that they should be aware of how their perception changes either as a result of the new information or because of hearing each other's reactions. '*Perhaps they can record such observations...*' Also warn them that they are 'going public' on this interview, in that all the other teams will watch.

You may consider that they need help with the *form* of the role-play. There are a number of unexpected aspects they need to understand. Clearly two of the four will be involved in representing the witness and interviewer. The third member of the team will take written notes, recording the words used in the interview. The fourth member has the most demanding task, as s/he will be the 'filter' through which learning occurs. The responsibility for effective learning does indeed rest on the fourth member's shoulders. The task is to monitor the interview from the point of view of what makes effective interviewing. It is her responsibility actually to stop the interview if there is anything she feels the onlookers could usefully discuss – aspects such as rushing the witness, showing appropriate degree of empathy, not really listening, not picking up on implied information or a gap in information, appropriateness of vocabulary, digressing, usefully or otherwise. The tone of this interruption is not to criticise negatively, although the way we have written it here may sound like it! It is to draw attention to skills needed in this kind of situation. Of particular interest is how perception, empathy or stance can change in the light of additional information.

Step 11

Not being actors, the officers playing 'the witness' may feel very vulnerable, unless you show them how to *indicate* the role without trying to 'get into the part':

You should demonstrate how it might be done by asking for a volunteer from the group to interview you for the rest to watch. Your concentration will be on finding answers that logically fit the questions and the picture of 'what happened last night'. You can add things as a witness would but they must not contradict anything that you know is in the written reports or on the extra information on the card – which you show to the audience before the interview begins. You do not try to impersonate a woman [if you are a man!] or put on a performance of being anxious. Nevertheless, and this is the tricky bit to get right, you allow yourself to be sufficiently part of the interview not to work against its 'truthfulness', its 'authenticity'. You will also look out for an opportunity to break off the proceedings to draw attention to how well or badly something was handled by 'the interviewer', reminding your class that when they do their prepared versions, this will be the responsibility of the fourth member of each group.

There is another aspect to this kind of work related to the use a 'space' in the room you are using. Too much space or too formal a space are both threatening. The above exercise, along with others we suggest, requires an *intimacy*. If I am a spectator, I am not going to find the right voice for speaking across space in order to comment or try to give helpful advice. And my voice will *sound* all wrong to the two participants – it will sound as though I'm addressing a meeting! Your observers will have to be *near* enough, so that a mere *leaning forward* will be sufficient for them and the participants to feel that the demonstration is really a shared problem.

Give time for discussion after your demonstration as to how you played your role and suggest they might for a few moments like to adjust what they have prepared in the light of the interview they have just observed.

Step 12

Each team of four in turn carries out the interview with the fourth member stopping it for comment or discussion.

When they are over, you should give the teams chance to go back into their own foursomes for the one who has been recording the dialogue

> to go over any points s/he want to raise. What happened in other groups may also be an important discussion point.

Presumably a lot of points will have been raised about interviewing during this role work and you may see it as a ripe moment for going over the the 'in house' guidelines on the subject or even introducing the usual lecture given on 'official' policy on interview procedures, especially relating to tone and manner – and give a hint that their understanding of these recommendations may well be put to the test in the next role exercise!

Step 13

Reminding them that this is not an exercise in solving a crime but an opportunity for observing what affects our perception of people. You now arrange a second interview:

You tell the teams that: '*a phone call has been made to the station by Mrs. James saying that she has seen the 'loiterer' in the fish shop and neighbours think they know where he lives.*' You give out four photographs or pictures cut from a magazine (one image to each team) showing an outside view of the place the 'loiterer' lives in – a smart semi-detached with neat front garden; a council house (glimpse of next door boarded up); student hostel; a flat over a shop.

> You hand one of the pictures to each team face downwards, telling them that when they turn it over (at a given instruction by you) they will see the home of the 'loiterer'. As soon as they see the picture they are separately to write down as fast as they can their expectations of the kind of person they are about to meet [1 minute allowed!]. They then, in turn, read out to each other what they have written, beginning with '*I expect the 'loiterer' will be...*' And then, choosing the descriptions common to all four lists, a spokesperson for each group will read out to the rest of the class: '*We expect our 'loiterer' to be...*'. You then discuss 'stereotyping' with your class, inviting them to suggest other signs we tend to use to stereotype people – colour; clothes, age group; make-up; accent; locality we see them in; their choice of car; their choice of dining out place; what they carry etc. Make list on flip-chart.

Step 14

You now organise the second interview, suggesting two different team members represent the 'loiterer' and 'interviewing PC'. The 'loiterer' is told that his name is Keith Eldon; he notes where he lives and takes in the extra information shown privately by you to him/her. The latter reads:

> You have nothing to do with the crime and did not see the men in the car

The 'PC' is to mentally prepare for the interview and you hope s/he may be conscious of already in her mind adapting her style to the photo she has seen of the witness's accommodation. So, four Keith Eldon's are interviewed. [If you prefer, because you are short of time or because the point is becoming laboured, or because the first set of 'public' demonstrations seemed inhibiting, to have the interviews conducted simultaneously, with the outcomes merely described to the whole class, but your objectives are more likely to be reached if each demonstration is shown separately]. Afterwards, the class will discuss both the influence of the pictures and the apparent effect of the earlier 'lecture'. Of course they will all, including the 'PC interviewer', be dying to know whether Keith Eldon, whom they will have seen protesting his innocence throughout the four interviews is guilty or not. You may care first to invite the views of the interviewers – and you ask them to justify their hunches. All they had to go on was the 'loiterer's' denial and explanation of why he was outside the Post Office, so, you all ask, is any part of that 'hunch' based on 'stereotype reading'? You then ask the whole class for their separate conclusions – treat this way of concluding quite lightly – and allow for laughs when they guess wrongly or guess right for the wrong reasons – the message will go home through, and even because of, the laughter.... Finally, give them time in their own teams for the 'scribe' to go over his/her record of the interview, particularly noting the extent to which the 'property' or 'the location' visited appeared to influence the conclusion.

[You may find that these last two interviewing practices are proving fruitful in which case you can 'arrange it' that the car has been traced and so they are able to interview its owner who 'cannot remember where s/he was on the night in question'. You may also gauge the extent to which you want this third interview practice to have a racist or anti-police dimension. If you do try a third interview then it would be inappropriate to have allowed the second one to turn into a 'fun' diversion of trying to guess whether or not the witness was involved – such trivialising would have to wait!]

You can point to the list made up by the class above of the signs we invariably use to stereotype people – your class has just used one based on where people live. One kind of sign they are unlikely to have included, which you can now add to the flip-chart list is the way we all tend to stereotype a *group* of people. We may be made to feel uneasy by their 'groupness': It may be simply because they *are* a group or it may be, to our way of thinking, there is something unconventional about them. For example:

A queue of youngsters outside a wine bar on a Saturday night

A lay-bye on a dual carriageway and five men are praying – outside their car, facing Mecca

A group of Romany people beside their horse drawn caravan

A picnic of 'special needs' adults

A group of people animatedly using deaf sign language

A group of shaven-headed youths eating fish and chips

Orthodox Jews gathering outside their synagogue on a Saturday.

A laughing and screaming group of 'jolly housewives'

etc etc.

Give one or two examples and make a list with your class. Just as you looked earlier at the five levels of values behind picking up or dropping litter, invite your class to detect what values lie behind a 'groupness'. Four deaf people might have widely different personalities but it is the handicap they have in common that makes them as one body of people, sharing *in this respect* a belief system:

Action: we are signing
Motivation: so that we can communicate
Investment: we can communicate uninhibitedly without feeling stupid
Cultural Model: others like ourselves
This is how life is: we accept that we are isolated by our handicap

Step 15

Go over an example with your whole class, writing down each level on the flip-chart, and then:

Introduce the idea of a ritual. Invite four volunteers to stand in the middle of the class who form a circle round them. You ask them to stand as four deaf people signing animatedly. You say *'Freeze!'*. They 'hold' their positions, while you invite the people round to write down derogatory, offensive remarks: *'Don't they look daft'*; *'They sound daft too, those funny grunts'*; *'They're deaf and dumb, you know – dumb's the word!'* etc. You may find a powerful reluctance in your group to join in this 'game' – it goes against their natural dispositions, so you must word your instruction very carefully. You might say *'...write down now the kinds of abusive things **you've heard said**...'* or *'...what are some of the worst things that could be said... if you wanted to abuse these people?...'* – so they work in pairs on this, one writing down the phrases – and you make a point of joining in by jotting down your own ideas. After a few moments you ask them to read out what has been written.

Then introduce the idea of a ritual, explaining that the phrases they have just read are going to be the opening lines. Warn the 'demonstrators' that they will be holding their still picture for a long time. Four from the circle will stand behind the four participants. Five others will stand in a line in front of the 'picture' – you hand each a card on which is a question (see below). When the abusive phrases are re-read, in turn, the ones in front will *formally* ask the five questions and the four behind will answer chorally, the four 'in the picture' remaining still and silent.

Question	Answer
What are you doing?	We are signing
Why are you doing that?	So that we can communicate
Why is it important to you?	We can communicate uninhibitedly without feeling stupid
Where did you learn to do that?	We learnt to do this from others like ourselves
How is life for you?	We accept that we are isolated by our handicap

You may find that this sequence is worth repeating, first the abusive comments, then quietly and smoothly moving into place, with all the dignity they can muster they speak their lines. The 'choral' aspect may need more practice.

You now invite each team to select another group from the list and prepare the dialogue, writing their chosen 'answers' down on cards which are to be placed behind [on the floor or pinned to the back of the participants] the 'still picture'. On a long strip of card to be placed in front of the presentation the participants write e.g.

We are orthodox Jews collecting at the synagogue on a Saturday

The teams cannot this time 'practise' the full ritual, so it may help if the class knows that each example will be gone through twice. It is the juxtaposition of abuse and statement of deep belief that is compelling and worth repetition to get it right. At some stage, the lines of the 'chorus' should be written up very large and placed somewhere prominent, especially if the room being used is one your officers may return to informally – so that their eyes can again, later, be caught with 'the wording they chose' – and be pondered on.

If, for the sake of smoothness, you made the mistake of asking them spontaneously to insult 'the group' with derogatory remarks, the effect might be right in its effect, but harmful to the individual. It would be too direct, too personal, to closely associated with a particular officer, too open to teasing in the canteen afterwards! What is needed is the *distancing* device of writing remarks down as if they are a script. And then, simply treating them as a script to be read out as part of practising the ritual. You hope that there will be some sense of having created something worthwhile at this point in your course. And then...

'How do the public see four police officers standing together?' you might suddenly drop in, if you feel that the previous exercise has caught their attention. *'If we were to be the group in the ritual... what abusive remarks might we invite?'* You are testing the ground here. If you sense the temperature of the room has dropped, shrug your shoulders as if you were making a passing remark before going on to something else, but if the invitation catches on and one or two risk saying aloud the kind of insult they are used to suffering, then you

might consider proceeding with... '*Could we invent our own ritual of values?*' If they show interest, ask them to work on it in their teams, deciding what the typical 'action' is that requires four of them to be seen together, trying out the 'still picture' and then writing the script of answers to the four remaining ritualistic questions.

Step 16

This exercise will only be of value to them if they are able to come up with a worthwhile 'belief system' for them as professional police officers. In particular, their choices for answers to 'What is life for you?' must have bearing on the defining character of being a police officer, its responsibilities, its ethical code, its cultural iniqueness. They may suddenly find they are not able to handle this in which case be prepared to turn it into a whole class exercise with you leading from the flip-chart, as it were. On the other hand, if you are at hand as they start their separate team work, encouraging, complimenting, adding a point here and there, they may achieve something worth setting on its feet. Again, the final ritualistic presentation must bring dignity to what they stand for. Less than this, means they are not ready and you have misjudged.

You are now reaching the point of winding up the short course. Here is a chance for the participants to give some shape to some aspects of their own work that they may have seen in a slightly different light as a result of the exercises. Some things will have remained half understood; some will soon be forgotten; others they will have rejected. The final exercise will go some way to pull together what has been going through their minds and linking it with aspects of their responsibilities the course has not managed to cover.

Step 17

The idea for this final exercise is for them to prepare a television documentary which will include 17 minutes of 'police officers talking about their responsibility to the community'. Your class may by now be feeling a bit whacked. One great reviver of concentration will be the presence of a video recorder, brought in to actually record their prepared 17 minutes.

You will explain that you will be in role as 'the programme presenter' who will ask very broad questions such as

'What would you say a police officer's priorities are?'...

'What are the rules of being a police officer that you become aware of when you first join the force?'

'How would you describe the pressures you are put under?'

'What steps do you take to improve the image of policing?'

'How aware are you of the ethnic minorities in your locality – and how do you learn about them?'

You now give time to your officers, perhaps working in pairs, to prepare the kind of thing they want to say in answer to these questions. Apologise for not giving them enough time for a polished presentation. Warn them that you might drop in supplementary questions, but that you have no intention of putting them on the defensive – this programme is to show the force at its best.

For the 'programme' arrange a shallow semi-circle of *eight* chairs for the 'interviewees' – the other eight will be out of camera range, monitoring the answers and noting the body language of those listening. Half-way through, break off the videoing so that 'speakers' and 'monitors' can change roles.

When time is up, invite self-criticism and comments arising from the 'monitors'' notes. Congratulate your class and leave the suggestion in the air that others could now learn from the video-tape they have made.

Indeed 'how others might learn' might well be uppermost in your mind. Here are 16 officers who have had a two-day course. Is there any way of their passing on what they have picked up from the course to their colleagues? Could each team of four be set the responsibility of passing something on to another four? Or, more specifically, could a package be prepared for taking into the upper classes (with ethnic mix) of secondary schools which includes a video of police officers 'being fair' in a racist context? Or, in another direction, should there be a Step 18 to finish the course, in which your officers are invited, in their teams, to prepare a brief 'mission statement' of policing, one that would particularly appeal to likely candidates from ethnic minorities?

Professor Williams[3] said in the 1997 Reith Lecture, entitled 'The Geneology of Race... Towards a Theory of Grace':... my subject has been small aggressions of unconscious racism, rather than big-booted oppressions of bigotry in its most extreme manifestations. I have chosen to speak of these quieter forms of racism because I think that the eradication of prejudice, the reconciling of tensions across racial, ethnic, cultural and religious lines depends upon eradicating the little blindnesses, not just the big.'

We hope that in this suggested course with the police on stereo-typing and our earlier discussion of how to educate young childen away from any incipient racist attitude, we have managed to shift 'little blindnesses' towards a more generous seeing.

Perhaps this indeed is a good definition of all role work, that we can claim our book has tried to find a form of practice that can move us towards 'a more generous seeing'.

References

1 Dated 20th May, 1999

2 *Prison Witness* 1986 by Tom Hadaway, Iron Press, Password Books Ltd., p6.

3 From the BBC Reith Lectures 1997, Lecture 5 'The Geneology of Race... Towards a Theory of Grace', Password Books Ltd., p6.

CHAPTER 8
PRACTICAL ISSUES, LEADER TAKING A ROLE AND LEARNING OUTCOMES

In this final chapter we will attempt to give some tips on practical issues. We follow with advice on the use of leader-in-role. Finally we pose the question: 'What do you want them to learn?' We try to summarise all the learning outcomes that role-work can help to bring about.

Some Practical Issues

There is a sense in which, in spite of the liberal scattering of examples throughout the book, it is only in the last chapter, 'Role-work with Police – stereotyping', that we give the reader a 'real' example. This plan for a two-day course comes off the page as material ready to be tested in a 'real' event, whereas many of the previous exercises lie in a vacuum as examples of what you might do *if you were* working with a particular subject-matter – and such examples, if used, would somehow still have to be slotted into 'real' practice for them to be given life. Nevertheless we hope that such examples will have been sufficient to demonstrate what might be called the 'laws' of role-work.

As a way of reinforcing much of the theory and practice of the whole book, however, we now will go through the Police course on stereotyping – reminding, elaborating, restating and linking some of those key 'laws'.

It is not difficult to imagine the apprehension that might be shared by a group of Officers directed to attend a course linked with

Racism. We suggested in Chapter Three that the central dimension of role work was to get the balance right between threatening and challenging. If ever a context illustrated the need for sensitivity, this group and this topic may be near the top of the league. 'Role-play' may already be a dirty word and for it to be linked with *racism...!*

Do the unusual, introductory steps (to do with 'throwing litter') meet the required balance? They certainly represent an unconventional way of starting a two-day workshop. We can think of a number of traditional role-play experts who would automatically feel inclined to start with 'games' – to break down barriers. You no doubt have noticed that 'games' have not played much of a part in this book. We have occasionally dropped one in to reinforce something that has been learnt. See, for example, A13 (p.12) in which we introduce a Board Game to help 9/10 year olds understand police duties relating to Road Safety, but we never introduce games with a view to 'relaxing' the participants. For we believe that, in its own curious way, a groups' success with an exercise as *intellectually* demanding as thinking through the 'levels of motivation' [Action; Motivation; Investment; Cultural Model; and This is how life is] allows the group to become more at ease with themselves. When they realise 'we can do *this*', there can be a mixture of relief, achievement, curiosity, trusting leader, trusting each other and trusting the material – a more productive attitude than 'mere' relaxing, for once you have spent time playing games, you *then* have to set to to arouse thoughtful application to the material.

We are not of course suggesting that this particular intellectual exercise should always be your starting point [nor that games should *never* be used to relax a group]. Indeed we doubt whether either of us has ever started a session with just that exercise, but what we are recommending is that whatever you start with should have that *bite* of intellectual promise – your class can both 'relax' and 'alert themselves' as they taste success with whatever the material is.

In this particular session you deliberately put yourself on the spot by demonstrating an action – picking up litter. This is theatre! Suddenly, a little bit of space and you doing something in it, has become significant because you said 'Watch this'. Had you picked up that toffee paper right under their noses without seeking their attention, they would not have 'seen' you. You had to indicate that 'this next moment is going to use special time' and 'this area of space is going to become special space' – and *then* you have made theatre. You even bring in 'scenery' and 'props' – the two chairs representing the garden fence and the half-eaten food.

Additionally, you have tacitly become a model for them to emulate throughout the course. You have made yourself vulnerable by saying 'Stare at me'. You may recall that we similarly begin our work with apprentice gas fitters (D1 p.38) when the leader begins: '*This chair is my driving seat... here's my bag of tools... etc*'. Now it is only actors, cookery demonstrators, preachers and politicians etc who professionally give such permission. People who are directed to attend courses have not. You will have noticed that most of our exercises, including the ones on the Police course, have built-in protective devices to reduce the 'staring'.

You want your class to take part in theatre and yet you want to protect them from exposure to staring. One way of doing both is to show how theatre requires the 'reading' of a *whole* context. When you sit in the 'headteacher's study' to be dressed down by the head for your alleged racism, the scene can only be understood in the light of the placard you are grasping in front of you with its 'This is how life is (for me)' phrase written large. Both you and the 'head' are protected by this notice, because the 'staring' becomes directed to-wards the mixture of reading, seeing and hearing: it is the interaction of signs that the class are to concentrate on. You are beginning to establish that attention to *meaning* and not attention to individuals is what the course is about.

Of course the 'staring' is of a particularly intense kind, because it intitiates not merely tasks but a 'point of view' and predicates an investment in outcomes which the 'starers' know they can influence.

Two kinds of writing occur in our exercises throughout the book – and they are a central activity to Role work. The first occurs in Step One. You ask for ideas from your class and write down their answers on a flip-chart. There are two ways of doing this. You can either write down everything they say or, as in this particular case, get some class agreement and then write it down. There are times when writing every suggestion preferably on a large blackboard is favourable, to be followed by a grouping of ideas and then a final selection. The purpose is to honour what they say. Each person sees that his contribution matters, and, of course, when someone answers 'tongue in cheek' *that* answer goes down too, given equal weight with the rest. It is astonishing how some glib suggestion, seen in a different light, can suddenly become relevant.

The other form of writing is for the participants. We would instil this habit early in the course (and, with children, at a very early school age) that any dramatising session automatically requires a handy pen and note-book. The major learning can occur during this time of recording or preparation or reflection or comment-making. In Step Two, the Police officers are invited to work in pairs or fours, typically setting up such writing as a *shared* activity. More than that, it defines **who they are** and manifestly plays down their role as a conventional audience to a performance. They are 'recorders' or 'analysts' or 'jotters of ideas' or 'self-spectators', never a passive audience. Schools can build an ethos of 'active spectatorship', but adult training courses depend on establishing the method as early as possible in the short course. (An interesting exception, of course, is the 'Performing Arts' or 'Drama' class in a Secondary School where it is important to have an audience function as a conventional audience. On the other hand, the idea of an audience as 'commenting' or 'recording' may be a godsend to English teachers who find themselves handling the performance of texts in their classroom as a way of studying them.)

So, how should you arrange the seating for role work? The readiness to slip into their pairs or teams of four should *override* any other arrangement. It is possible that many people reading Step One have visualised some rows of participants facing a leader who stands at 'the front' with flip-chart and from there demonstrates the 'litter' incident. We suggest you might consider starting in a circle or $3/4$ circle, so that you are all facing each other, making it easier to 'pair off' and to slip into a 'team of four' – *and back again* to the circle to discuss as a whole group or watch the next demonstration. This is why we limited the class to 16, a number that also lends itself to a nicely balanced four 'teams of four'. The circle or $3/4$ circle also create that degree of intimacy necessary by the time they reach Step 10 where the observers are sufficiently near to 'lean in' to interrupt a scene if something worth commenting on crops up.

The emphasis on intimacy creates a sense of 'working together', but does not necessarily provide the protection the participants need at times. What begins within the circle as 'slipping into fours' for sharing a discussion needs more space and physical separation from other teams as the course progresses, especially when they are required as in Step Two to prepare a demonstration that others are going to watch. At this point they need privacy and the feeling that no-one is watching or listening. And you will probably find them shuffling their chairs into corners, and, of course, the 'returning to the circle' when needed will by then have been well established.

You have to strike a delicate balance during these preparation periods between, at worst, showing no interest in what they are doing and, again at worst, interfering because you really know best. There are all sorts of subtle variations in the way you might give support without appearing to distrust. One way (to be used occasionally) is to be seen making your own 'list' or 'plan' or whatever and to be heard muttering *'This is harder than you'd think... I wonder what people are doing about...?'* If, on the other hand you choose to 'hover' at the edge of each group, you might say something like, *'Can I share with you how I am reading what you are saying (or doing)...?'*

The first few steps require one volunteer Police officer to take a role and share the demonstration with you. This is quite a risk, for such a volunteer can set the tone for the rest. S/he may feel so self-conscious that s/he resorts to 'entertaining' or indulges in *'I can't think what to say...'* If you feel there is a danger of this happening, it may help if you invite the whole group to suggest 'headteacher' or 'police' questions, so that the volunteer is virtually reading a script. Or it is possible, but this creates a different kind of challenge, to treat the whole group as *a* character, as *a* headteacher or police officer, so that that character's question can come from anywhere in the circle and you respond as if you are facing *one* other person.

This latter format is very useful if the subject-matter is emotionally distressing. For instance, Gavin Bolton once in role as a doctor, had to announce to a parent that as a result of the motor-byke accident her son would emerge from the operation severely brain damaged. Such a scene, if it is to ring 'true' would have been too disturbing for everyone; if it fell short of 'true', it would be embarrassing. So a *formalising* of the parent's character removes the responsibility to 'make it seems real' – and yet, the voices of the parent coming from different points in a semi-circle in front of 'the doctor' carried the authentic questions. We were all aware of the distress without having to simulate it.

Step Nine requires a major stride forward from this use of but one volunteer. The exercise in fours to plan and demonstrate an interview tests their commitment to the course. Notice the 'way in' to the task – through written material. Police officers are accustomed to having to visualise an incident through a written account. It is a common form of communication in this particular profession, so you are inviting them to use skills they already have as their first approach to role-play. Compare this with the way in chosen for the trainee doctors for whom a written report would have been a reminder of what they *don't know*. The level of task for the latter trainees merely related to what a doctor would typically carry or what a daily routine would look like. Sometimes reading-matter is necessarily the starting point. English Lit students *must* start with the text, even though one might do all sorts of activities that temporarily move away from it. You will have noticed in the chapter on 'Sign' (Chapter 4, p.98) how a difficult text can be cut up, spread round the walls or floor, highlighted to focus attention, and their reading sharpened by a search for the answer to something.

Step Nine sets your class off on preparing the demonstration, but once more you give them a 'model' of the kind of behaviour required by the 'actors'. As we suggested in Chapter 3 (p.68), it is important to model the level at which enactment should be pitched. It is as if you were saying: 'Supposing it were *thus...*', not the 'pure' present tense of 'it is happening now', but a subjunctive tense, opening up something to be considered.

Step 15 takes you into a different kind of theatre form, that of ritual. Ritual, because of its formal use of space and time, allows you to use dialogue that could not in normal interactions ever be voiced. We hardly ever speak our deepest values (indeed, we may not be aware of them) and yet they are just what we want to give recognition to. Attempting to bring dignity to the relative positions of bodies and to the use of gesture, combined with the deliberate slowing down of speech and the introduction of words chorally spoken, permits the introduction of abstract concepts.

Step 17 is our only example with the Police Force's two-day course of the use of leader-in-role, and it is about the most straightforward of its kind, in that you will simply be continuing to do in role [i.e., ask questions] what you have been doing throughout the session. All you have done is indicate that you will be 'a programme presenter'. In spite of its similarity with 'real life', there will be important differences that point to the way leader-in-role or teacher-in-role functions. Your class will see you abiding by a new set of rules that belong to the fictional context. You will adopt a courtesy of an interviewer asking questions of strangers; your role of 'outsider to the police' allows you to 'not understand' an answer and ask for amplification; you will give the impression of a professional who is used to restrictions of broadcasting to do with timing and sustaining the interest of viewers; you will key them into their roles; and convey the ambience of a studio. Above all your class will see you operating with two viewpoints, as their leader having their learning and security as your priority and as a programme presenter getting the best out of them for the sake of the public. Typically of this technique, it is this juxtaposition of viewpoints that uniquely gives the participants a fresh perspective on what they are learning. Role work is about repositioning oneself in respect of some subject-matter. When the leader is in role, that shift of position has already begun for the learners.

Sometimes such usage is much more subtle and demanding. Let us look at leader-in-role in more detail:

Leader-in-role

If we look back at the section (p.102) in which students were to learn about the design of the Globe Theatre, one of our paragraphs reads as follows:

> But if you want them to be arriving to *train* as guides, then you have to convey that you don't know anything about that 'scholarship stuff' – you're a manager not a scholar, but you assume the applicants can 'mug it up' before it opens in a few months time *'Mind, they'll have to get a move on... we're supposed to be open to the public in three months... the builders can't let us wander round... but I've got these plans from the architect... they're only copies... so you can write on them if you have to... this'll be your common room, by the way... it'll have a notice on the door... but you're lucky to have the room... the actors can't get in the theatre yet to rehearse... you better wear these badges by the way else someone will want to know what you're doing here... there's coffee over there...'* They can only have artists' impressions, architect's plans and photographs, so you will have to convey that they are not allowed to enter the stage area of the new structure yet, to have a look at it.

Here your role has to convey a whole range of facets – *who* your class are; *what* their job is; *where* they are – a room in a theatre that's partly in the build and is to be occupied by other people; what restrictions of movement there are; that it is a particular point in the building's history; that there is some sort of deadline; who *you* are and that there's coffee on tap!; And if that isn't enough, you begin, through your role, to *teach* them what they need to know as guides:

> All your initial signing will be businesslike and 'cool'. You will have already added comments or labels to parts of the drawings on display, indicating accurate information about the placings and measurements [modern, of course] of trapdoors for 'ghosts and 'gravediggers' – sufficient of these to grab the attention of the class when they do their first browsing. It is while they are browsing that you verbally build background information that they are going to need... *'...they must have had good timbers to support all those balconies and storeys... we're on the fourth floor up here!... they seem to think this building'll be the nearest there's ever been to an accurate replica of the Globe...'*

[We seem with this 'Globe theatre' example to have advanced considerably on your becoming a 'programme presenter' to a class of Police Officers!]

There is a feature of the 'theatre design' role-play that should not be overlooked. In endowing the class with their role, it is significantly a *collective* role, not in the sense of their being one character, as in the 'motor-byke' tragedy cited above, nor in the sense used in the Police example in which the leader-in-role allowed for the participants to retain their individualism, but in its effective establishment of a *group* of people. A typical usage at the beginning of a session, whether it is teacher waving a spoon at her infants and saying: *'Line up for school dinner...'* (p.76) or a teacher as a worried parent saying *'Has anyone seen K...?'* (A4. pp.3-4) or, as above, the theatre manager addressing the students as 'trainee guides', creates a 'groupness' first, so that collectively they learn who they are, their responsibilities to the fiction and their first shared task. And then, as it seems right to do so, individuals may emerge. It may be this aspect of leader-in-role that marks it as of paramount educational importance. The fiction is established and the group's role in it at one fell swoop and far from being in the *subjunctive* tense of a demonstration, it is in the *present* tense of 'it is happening now' – but it is happening to a homogeneous *group*, initially requiring a *group* response. This is what gives it its power.

All the way through this publication we have emphasised the importance of protecting your trainees, students or pupils. We have not given much attention to protecting *you*! To some extent we have assumed that you already have some of the negotiating skills of a course leader and we have given a lot of advice on how to structure an exercise, how to introduce activities to your groups, how to win their trust etc. What we have not done, is discuss how you might prepare yourself for leading-in-role.

Unless you are very experienced, the prospect of playing a role as complex in its objectives as the Globe Theatre manager described above must be quite alarming. Fortunately, that degree of elaboration is rarely needed. Most leader-in-role work requires a *token* sign and but one or two objectives. And yet, it must be faced, many of us have a deep fear of taking on a role in public, let alone a role that is to endow others with their role. Let us, before giving advice, consider why this might be the case.

Whenever, in 'real' life, we address a group of people, we draw on our 'social' role, the one (and most of us have only one!) that we adopt when we are to make a speech (at a wedding, say) or bring up a point we want to argue at a meeting, or, if we are in education, instruct a class. We have acquired our 'social' role over the years (and there are many for whom refinding it when it is needed requires nerve) and, having acquired a 'public face' that works, the last thing we want to do is risk finding a different one. And 'leader or teacher-in-role' requires us to do just that.

One function of our 'social role' is to confirm the social context and reaffirm who the listeners are. The 'Best Man', the speaker from the floor at a meeting, and the teacher all legitimise what is going on. However, the nervous 'best man', speaker, and teacher, *undermine* the legitimacy of what is going on and the listeners are unnerved by uncertainty. The social role must carry conviction – as must the role that a leader adopts to create a fiction. You say to your Police Officers *'Let me introduce myself, I am the programme presenter... and I will be interviewing you...'* – and they know they are not in a TV studio, that you are not a presenter and that it's not a 'real' interview. No wonder even the most experienced leaders baulk at being in role, for they feel they have to find a role as convincing and as acceptable as their normal 'social role' – but this is to misunderstand what is required.

You will need skills, but not the skill of a performer. Whatever form your 'normal' social role takes with the class you are working with will be retained, clearly visible, and your class see you using 'quotation marks', as it were. Your *'Let me introduce myself, I am the pro gramme presenter...'* should be heard as you quoting a programme presenter. Your whole demeanour – you may have become more serious, more officious, more business-like etc. – should be seen as a quotation, but, of course, such a demeanour is present now and your words are expressed in the present tense, so the *feeling* is of 'it's happening now', in so far as you choose it to be... Thus it would be quite in order, should you choose, to say '*Let me introduce myself, I am the programme presenter...*' [I wouldn't mind his salary!...] *...'...and I will be interviewing you...*' You deliberately include 'two' voices as a way of saying, 'We are not pretending to be real'. But, of course, you are trying to make it *truthful* to the context and the presentation of these two voices simultaneously requires *authoritative* handling. This is where the skill lies, not in your acting ability but in your confidence to present two voices. Further than this, it is in the nature of this 'game' that as people enjoy playing it, yours and their 'social roles' need less and less reinforcing. They are always tacitly present, but do not need to be given attention. Thus part of your skill is to recognise the point when the only 'signing', verbal and non-verbal, needed lies within the quotation marks. You may find that in working with groups experienced in role-work or absolutely committed to the subject-matter, you need not continue to make the 'social role' explicit at all.

With an inexperienced group you may choose, before you start, to make a contract and say: '*Will you agree that we are in a studio... and I am behaving as a programme presenter... so that your police expertise can reach the viewers at home...?*' Another useful way of ensuring that your class understand about 'two voices' is for them to have some responsibility in creating your fictional role. In chapter 5 (p.122) we give an example of 'Mantle of the Expert' approach to teaching Science in a Junior school. At one point in the sequence (taking place over at least a term) a visit is required from 'the Secretary to the Cardiff National Gardens Festival' – a role that will be played by the class teacher, who invites the class to invent the kind of person they want 'Owen Evans' to be. Thus before this 'visit', the class teacher finds herself saying: '*Do you want him to be a chap who doesn't miss a trick... who's done his homework... or a guy who couldn't care less... who's going to have to be taught...*' and so on. [Notice that the choice is a narrow one between two options. Although not applicable in this case, with some classes, because of a negative social health one would not risk giving an open-ended choice, as you could be landed with a role that was impossible or embarrassing!]. And when 'Owen Evans' arrives, the pupils will engage with the two voices (using 'voice' in its broadest sense to include non-verbal signalling) of class teacher and 'role'. And they will *enjoy* the combination and enjoy the 'game'.

It is when you see the enjoyment your class gets out of engaging with the two voices that you will fully appreciate that whether or not you could be a 'good' actor in the traditional sense is irrelevant.

Summarising the whole book – so what do you want them to learn?

Throughout this book we have stressed the importance of extending or deepening the understanding of the participants. Indeed there appears to be little value in any classroom practice unless new learning takes place. From the exercises in role-work given in the previous chapters it seems that either the role-play itself may bring about a change of perspective or it constructs a platform for developing a necessary, further stage of constructive reflection beyond role-play. Or these together.

But what is this *extending* or *deepening* or *new learning or change of perspective?* These are pretty vague terms. Can we make them a bit more concrete? Role-work 'does something' that other teaching strategies cannot achieve. This is an enormous claim, but we do indeed believe that its power is educationally far-reaching. That power broadly seems to derive from a combination of three dynamics: (1) the obvious one of its being a *shared* learning. There is an inclusivity that both energises and supports; (2) that it stimulates in the participants a vested interest derived from a 'point of view'; and (3) the self-spectatorship brought about by (2) What appears to be about something else is really about 'me'. When the infant children make their condolence cards and take them to the grieving parent, they do so with a high degree of shared motivation, a compulsion that creates its own alertness to learning. Similarly, if at the end of a successful two-day course with the Police Officers, they were invited, say, to write a mission statement, the dynamics of inclusivity and self-aware commitment would impel them towards the task with a heightened degree of attention to what is needed.

If role-work can create this readiness for learning, it will help if we can find a simple classification for that learning. We have found six major categories:

1. The most concrete form of learning: practising behaviours

Where we feel we have a right to control behaviour, it is relatively simple to set up a role-play sequence that is going to give the participants practice in behavioural procedures. Such rote learning is usually necessary where circumstances must repeat themselves, where those who carry them out need to know exactly the procedure to follow. Such occasions deliberately subdue any idiosyncratic, personalised behaviour and provide a safety net of protection for staff and public – the formal dialogue a police officer is required to follow in making an arrest is a good example. Another example occurs when a large hotel trains its reception staff in a procedure for receiving and dealing with a complaint from a guest the other side of the desk. It may well be that the steps are to be:

1. You should request clarification without appearing to be hostile or critical.

2. Demonstrate, by restating the complaint, that you understand it [mentally, you are assessing its complexity and figuring out which part(s) of the hotel organisation are likely to be involved].

3. Find a way, without being patronising, of conveying your grasp of how upset the guest is over the problem.

4. State the hotel's policy on the issue.

5. Say what steps you intend to take to deal with the matter, apologising where that is appropriate.

Given that the leader grades the exercises according to complexity [in this case, from, say, a complaint about the bedroom being too cold to a complaint about the noise from children in the bedroom next door], learning will be a matter of practice within the safety of the role-play, coupled with critical observation from those who watched the role-play and, of course, 'real life' practice at the reception desk.

Similar exercises may be set up in a school context for staff who bear the responsibility of receiving pupils who are sent to them for bad behaviour in someone else's classroom – there could be guidelines laid down that created 'space' for assessing the problem while containing the distress of both pupil and teacher concerned – and (a much more tentative example) for pupils who are to be given guidance on how to handle 'name-calling' – a list of neutral behaviours such as 'ignoring', 'walking away', 'being pre-occupied with something else' or saying variations on 'I don't find that particularly funny' may be practised and tested.

There is always a second aspect to this 'procedure' practice – the procedure itself may be subject to scrutiny, so that commentators may assess not merely how an individual coped but the validity of the procedure.

Altogether this makes for a 'tidy' exercise. You know exactly what is to be learnt; you can instruct the observers precisely on what to look for. Behaviour modification of this type provides but one usage for role-play.

2. Acquiring information

Perhaps this limited form of learning represents the bulk of school learning. Role-play may reinforce what pupils already know or used to know, introduce information new to them or (and this is perhaps role-play at its most useful given the narrow scope of this kind of learning) help them to look at the information from an unusual angle. Let us look at an example of each of these:

> A language teacher may, having handed out lists of items of food typically to be found on a menu, may take the role of a waiter and ask class members what they would like to eat.

> A physiology teacher may give out a report on a patient's condition, a report containing technical terms new to the class, who are asked to speculate about treatment.

> After studying a play a class are 'hot-seated' by the teacher, who, addressing class members as if they are the characters from the play, seeks to know why they behaved as they did in the play, putting pressure on them to justify themselves while remaining true to the text.

This last approach where the material remains the same but the angle on it changes lies at the heart of role-play and takes us into the next area of learning.

3. Going beyond information

The above section, *acquiring information*, pragmatically assumes that information is static. It is sometimes convenient to think so. But most good teachers recognise that *understanding* is dependent on having an awareness of the *implications* of the information. Role-play is good at inviting the participants to look at *consequences* of holding [or withholding] that information, to recognise *imbalances in responsibilities* in holding that information, to consider *how that information might be communicated*. For instance:

> In 17th century Salem, Massachusetts, respectable citizens were accused of being witches. A still depiction, with voices over or commentary, can allow a group formerly to convey how individual citizens were affected by the pervading hysteria, how the church authorities garnered power, how people were secretive or spread rumours, how people were controlled by fear.

4. A training in how to enquire

We want the educated person to be able to ask the questions. It is not enough to have the information relating to an issue or even for a good leader to be able to pose the questions that will draw attention to the *significance* of that information. We want our students to be educated in knowing what questions to ask and to develop the habit of asking them. In other words there is a philosophical *procedure* that should be part of the educated person's armoury, whatever the topic, information or issue. That procedure largely revolves round the following three areas.

(a) The empirical question

Perhaps the first question we want to train our students to ask is: 'Is it true?'. When they view a role-play we want them to recognise that sometimes the facts of the material presented are incorrect and that they should habitually check.

(b) The conceptual question

Sometimes clarification has to be sought in how words are being used, either by the 'characters' or by everyone in the reflective discussion following the role-play. So when we hear one character accuse another of being 'stupid', we need afterwards to ask 'What does that character really *mean* by that? Does he mean 'feeble-minded' or 'obstinate' or unwise' etc or is he really conveying to us that *he* cannot cope with the other character's behaviour – his use of the word telling us more about him than the character he is addressing – or does he really mean 'I want a fight'? Likewise, if in discussing, say, Puritan Salem, we need to train our students not to just pass over the kind input to the discussion that fails to get beyond 'Those Puritans were stupid!'. Obviously a good *leader* will challenge this kind of conceptual inadequacy, but we want our *students* to initiate that challenging.

(c) The 'value' question

There appear to be two levels to this kind of probing. There is a moral/ethical question that is typically expressed as 'Did s/he do the right thing [in the role-play]' and 'How do we justify our conclusions?' There is a further question which accounts for a character's behaviour in cultural terms, which asks 'What are the tacit or explicit laws/rules in this character's culture or sub-culture that require/lead him to follow/choose this behaviour?' Our chapters on 'racism' moved into this area of understanding a person's deepest motives.

It is perhaps foolish to attempt to isolate any one question, but this recognition that behaviour may be, at least in part, culturally determined and that a person's set of values may be culturally derived is paramount in role-work. To understand their action, we may need to grasp something of that cultural influence and, further, to assess the extent to which s/he had a choice of action. Dramatisation more than any other artistic medium lends itself to giving answers to this kind of question and role-play, limited as it may be in other respects, retains this capacity for reflecting a hidden cultural dimension. All particpants in role-work should be taught to use this cultural probe if they are to get the most from role-play.

5. Attention to detail

The ability to ask the searching questions outlined above as empirical, conceptual and value-laden, is preconditioned by a disposition to give attention to detail. In most of our role-play exercises outlined in the earlier chapters, the classes are constantly required to scrutinise the written word or their own and other people's actions. Role work can help develop the habit of alertness to particulars, whether it be scrutinising a Shakespearean text, a report or a mission statement; or whether observing how an interview is conducted or an instruction carried out. Above all, it can generate in our students a pleasure in noting detail for its own sake – the basis of scholarship, communication and counselling.

6. Change in values or attitude

If we cast our minds back to 'road drill' in an infants school, here is an example in which practising something like 'look right; look left; and right again' is not in itself sufficient. In the above examples of behaviour modification it could be assumed that the participants in the role-work (hotel receptionists; teachers in charge of discipline problems and pupils vulnerable to bullying) had a vested interest in the practice. With 'road safety' we are hoping to teach our pupils to *care* about road drill; we want to, as it were, *give* them a vested interest. Behaviour modification can only be said to occur when the children have a heightened awareness of the subject matter as significant for *them*, when they acquire some sense of *responsibility* towards it. (Other examples, according to age and relevance, relate to drug-taking; smoking; safe sex; the citizen's duty to vote; importance of schoolwork; work ethic and so on.)

Thus for these topics the role-play must capture their imaginations sufficiently to enter their value systems. The outcome required is a change of perception and attitude. This is a huge advance on practising a prescribed sequence of behaviour. Dabbling in a role-play exercise or two is unlikely to effect such a fundamental change.

There are four avenues for bringing about a deeper change of behaviour or attitude:

(a) A *programme* of carefully sequenced steps, as we have illustrated with the Police stereotyping, where the aim is that the cumulative experience will have sufficient impact to help the participants re-think their position.

(b) Such a programme may include the 'making' of something. In the Road Safety the young children's entry into understanding grieving was the designing of condolence cards; the Northern Gas managers had to prepare an elaborate plan for the modernisation of 'Gongua'; and, as suggested above, the Police Officers could round their course off with the preparation of a 'mission statement'. Creating some kind of 'product' (usually a collective enterprise) in which significant values are implicitly embedded is a way of absorbing those values and 'owning' them without necessarily being able to articulate them.

(c) One of the limiting but necessary features of role work is that the deviser of the exercises retains control of the programme. Most of the work is short-term, each selected exercise having a limited objective. The 'police officer' two-day course is an example of a carefully (some might justifiably say 'rigidly'!) planned sequence. However, in schools that have drama as part of their curriculum, then 'play-making' in which a class, either as a whole or in small groups, can take responsibility for creating a drama, the outcome of which may not be clear from the beginning, has an important place. Now here is a totally different means of absorbing new values. It has not been within the scope of this book to discuss this kind of dramatic work which drama teachers will be familiar with, but we felt it is important for readers to at least be aware of it. We believe that it is this process of building their own play that may lead to an incorporation of its underlying values into pupils' own attitudinal profile. This is not an area for *ready-made* role-plays devised by the leader. This requires school students in a drama class to seek authentic material, to find a theatre form they are capable of handling, of shaping and refining and of showing to a critical audience. Thus the responsibility you hope they acquire towards some important issue or subject-matter has a chance of emerging from having taken on a responsibility for making a dramatic presentation.

(d) There is a fourth avenue for bringing about a deeper change in attitude, not necessarily confined to schools, which we have given but one brief example of – 'Mantle of the Expert'. On pages 122-128 we briefly show how Junior School pupils can engage with a Science project by becoming consultants to a Garden Festival. All we did in that example is give a *flavour* of 'Mantle of the Expert', which again has really been outside the scope of this book, for to carry out this kind of work properly demands that it be seen as an ongoing project over a long period of time, so that its inner values related to professionalism, responsibility and respect for accuracy become absorbed into the pupils' own life-style. It need not be confined to schoolwork. Dorothy Heathcote conducted such a project with Volkswagen managers. For readers attracted by this approach we recommend *Drama for Learning: Dorothy Heathcote's Mantle of the Expert Approach to Education.*[1]

Thus, in this chapter, we have attempted to summarise the the different kinds of learning outcomes to be derived from the use of role work. We have used the following headings:

1. Behaviour practice
2. Acquiring information
3. Beyond acquiring information to implications
4. Training in how to enquire
5. Attention to detail
6. Role work for change in values and attitude

And there is, of course, a seventh: Training in how to use role-work. We hope this book has gone some way towards this.

Reference

Dorothy Heathcote and Gavin Bolton *Drama for Learning: Dorothy Heathcote's Mantle of the Expert Approach to Education* Heinemann Portsmouth NH 1995

INDEX